MOTHERING UPSTREAM

MOTHERING UPSTREAM

VIRELLE KIDDER

VICTOR BOOKS ®

A DIVISION OF SCRIPTURE PRESS PUBLICATIONS INC.
USA CANADA ENGLAND

Library of Congress Cataloging-in-Publication Data

Kidder, Virelle.
   Mothering upstream / by Virelle Kidder.
     p.   cm.
   Includes bibliographical references.
   ISBN 0-89693-543-4
   1. Motherhood. 2. Child rearing—Religious aspects—Christianity.
I. Title.
HQ759.K52   1990
649′.1–dc20   90-41887
                                                               CIP

1 2 3 4 5 6 7 8 9 10 Printing/Year 94 93 92 91 90

CONTENTS

To my wonderful husband
Steve
whose companionship and love
have made these the best years of my life

and

to my four dear children
who love me anyway

P R E F A C E

Every year in August, the teenagers in our church turn out in great numbers for their favorite event of the year: the canoe trip! Four or five hardy adults are willing year after year to lead that noisy, irreverent group up the famous Oswegatchie River into the Adirondack wilderness for four glorious days. Our children look forward to it like Christmas. Methodically, they pack each day's change of clothes into its own sealed plastic bag, carefully labeled which day they will wear it. Of course, they all come home clean, bags unopened. Who changes their clothes on a canoe trip?

The tales of adventure, hilarity, stress, exhaustion, grit and grime that come from these canoe trips usually keep Steve and me spellbound for at least a week, nonstop. I wish I had recorded them on tape. You'd think, on first hearing, that it was an awful trip.

"You guys would never believe what we went through! Leeches in the river, running into rocks, I got tipped over and had to dive for all my gear! Then it rained steadily for three days. My sleeping bag never dried out. We had to cook in the rain, and it took forever to get the fire going. The food tasted pretty good, whatever didn't get burned, that is."

"Honey," I reply, amazed they made it home alive, "that sounds just terrible! I don't know how you made it through it. I bet you wish you had stayed home!"

"Are you crazy?" My teenager turns to me, incredulous, probably wondering how Mother could be such a block-head. "That was the best thing I ever did in my life! I wouldn't miss it unless I died! I LOVE the canoe trip!"

So much for communication in our family!

Mothering is a little like the canoe trip. Lots of challenges, a few necessary hardships, certainly a test of endurance, but oh, the joy of the ride, the beauty of it all, the thrill of reaching your destination! I wouldn't have missed it for the world!

Little needs to be said about all the joys of being a mother. Who needs help handling happiness and contentment? The purpose of this book is to offer a little boost over the hurdles and to hold out a vision for you to consider regarding the tremendous value in your role as a mother. I hope you will find encouragement here, help with some of the stickier problems, and an incentive to keep going that comes right from the heart of God.

Virelle Kidder
Schenectady, New York
1990

ONE

THE REAL TRUTH ABOUT MOTHERING

I'm her mother!" I argued, raising my voice a notch or two above normal. "It's my right to do it!" I insisted, reaching for the pair of tiny pink feet and spindly little legs suspended from Steve's left hand.

"But you got to do everything for her in the hospital. Now it's my turn!" Steve returned flatly, as he grabbed for the smelly diaper. Thus ended our first argument as parents, five minutes after arriving home from the hospital with our first baby, Lauren, twenty-three years ago. It absolutely eludes me now why I ever offered any resistance.

Raising children has proven itself such a different sort of task than I had ever imagined. As the younger of two children, I had never seen anyone else raised. The whole experience of motherhood was like an unexplored landscape. During my thirty-six-hour labor, one nurse spent her entire shift reading aloud to me long portions of Dr. Spock's *Baby and Child Care*, virtually my only preparation for mothering. I presumed that some combination of instinct and intellect would soon take over, that I could probably muddle through as well as the rest of them. My own resources soon proved too shallow for the task with sleepless nights spent wearing a circular path on the bedroom rug, trying to coax a wide-awake baby to sleep, fighting nausea after opening the diaper pail twenty times a day, feeling lonely, cooped up, and miserable in a three-room apartment all day and most of the evening while my husband attended graduate school.

Motherhood wasn't at all what I had dreamed about. With a determination to survive, and even love my new role in life, I became a hawkish observer of other mothers, and an avid reader on parenting in general. But of greater importance, within three years of Lauren's birth, I also became a Christian. Before me lay a whole new world — a world of comfort and guidance from the Scriptures, accountability to God and to others, and a challenge to view my present circumstances as God's plan for my life. He provided me with models who demonstrated motherhood with all the love, enjoyment, and sanity that He intended.

This book is an account of that sometimes heavy-duty journey in growth as a mother. It is designed to offer practical help and encouragement to those of you on the same path, especially if you find yourself struggling through the early years. For those who are perhaps feeling exhausted midstream, I hope it will inspire a second wind.

I have taken great comfort from the advice of a dear friend, Ruth Camp, now a perfectly delightful grandmother. After I poured out some complaint to her many years ago, she countered, "It's just fine if you're struggling, Virelle! There's nothing unspiritual about a struggle. In fact, that's exactly where God wants you, because you will lay hold of Him. He will meet you there and you'll never be the same again." That was some of the best advice I ever received, and it has proven very true. The pages that follow are the offering of all that God has been able to teach me about mothering through His Word, through experience, and in marvelous examples of women like Ruth.

God has entrusted to my husband, Steve, and me four fantastic children, each one totally unique. They have become our teacher/trainers in the school of loving and forgiving, faith and tenacity. Their lives have also taken us to new and frightening heights in parenting, like jumping off one precipice after another. The parachute of faith and the winds of grace have landed us, safe and unharmed, time and time again. Parenting four children with a wonderful husband has been one of the greatest joys of my life, but there have been issues and problems that were solely mine as a mother. Never would I suggest that a mother is all that is needed. But if Mom goes under, often the whole family follows. She is a central figure in the life of each family member, critical to their lifelong character, faith, and personal completeness.

Mothering is the long-term, usually upstream process that loves and launches children from the nursery to adulthood. Mothering is, by definition, feminine, and wonderfully so. It is one leg of two needed for a balanced home.

When done well, I believe mothering expresses God's character in a way nothing else can. He also nurtures those newly born to His family, surrounding them with the love of their new family in Christ, as He protects, teaches, guides, exercises their faith, and yes, disciplines. God is the perfect parent. We usually think of the Fatherhood of God, but He has chosen distinctly "mothering" terms to describe His relationship with His children: "As one whom his mother comforts, so will I comfort you" (Isaiah 66:13). And again in Luke 13:3-4 Jesus cries out, "O Jerusalem, Jerusalem . . . how often I have longed to gather your children together as a hen gathers her chicks under her wings, but you would not." Even being born of the Spirit suggests the motherhood of God.

We have only to look briefly at God's long-term upstream relationship with the Children of Israel to see that it wasn't all easy for Him, either. There were wonderful moments when their faith embraced His great love, but they were dwarfed by even more moments when God felt grief and despair over their foolish and rebellious ways. On one or two occasions, He nearly gave up. We shouldn't expect our own experience with our children to be without similar heights and valleys either. Every mother knows that laughter and tears are strange cousins. Joys that are most treasured follow on the heels of a long and sometimes sorrowful wait.

Every child God has entrusted to you is His perfect choice. There are no mistakes, whatever their particular problems and personality quirks. Often the biggest hurdle for mothers is simply thanking God for their children.

"But you just don't understand!" someone will complain. "My child is impossible; I can't manage him anymore. My patience is gone by noon!"

Another may feel she is simply not a natural at this and can find neither instinct nor inclination for mothering. Perhaps an unplanned pregnancy has left her with few inner resources to meet the twenty-four-hour challenge. Fear of the future and a feeling of confinement tempt her to give up.

Or how about the mother of a surprise midlife baby? Talk about a "grace grower"!

Regardless of your feelings at this moment, or who your children are, you are God's first and best choice to mother them, as an irreplaceable link in His plan. He will both equip you and make you able to fully carry out His plan. All of God's Word consistently promises this.

The Supermom Trap

One of the most common problems we mothers fall into is the trap of expecting total perfection from ourselves. Never raise your voice, always have cookies made, enjoy every moment you have at home with your children, read to them often each day. Be sure to look refreshed and striking when guests drop in unexpectedly or your husband comes home early for dinner. Lead a Brownie troop, be a homeroom mother, find time to sing in the choir, teach Sunday School, and take an exercise class twice a week.

How quickly we commend others, yet our own performance is never quite good enough. The Supermom trap is an elusive dream that turns quickly into a nightmare. But God, in His tremendous love, never expects such a worldly standard of perfection. He is aiming at something quite different, our loving faith and obedience to Him.

This understanding came unexpectedly to me one hot summer afternoon. I was washing the dishes while keeping a watchful eye out the sliding glass doors on the swingset, where my four children and a few others were playing. It was just past lunchtime, but already the day seemed much too long. Hot, cranky, and bored, the children seemed unable to share the swings or the toys in the sandpile. I had been settling disagreements all morning and was running low on patience.

As I wiped the last traces of peanut butter and jelly from the counter, I heard a long wail from outside, "Mommy! David won't get off the swing and he hit me!"

An emergency prayer came bursting out of my mouth, "Lord, I can't stand my children right now! Is there anything wrong with that?"

Spoken loud and clear to my heart came His reply, "I know exactly how you feel. I've felt the same way about My children before too! Just see that you don't sin."

Amazing! No condemnation! I cannot describe for you the comfort it gave me that hot afternoon, just to know that God understood me perfectly and cared. He didn't expect me to be a Supermom, but rather a loving and obedient child, the kind I was trying to raise. His loving understanding lightened my load, and His word of caution helped me see my need to depend on Him continually for fresh patience and love. What a wonderful God we have who accepts us as we are even on our worst days! We put enormous burdens on ourselves and everyone around us when we think we have the inner resources to be perfect. In his book, *Healing Grace*, David Seamands quotes someone who wisely said, "Perfectionists are those who take great pains and give them to others."[1] Right on! Only our Heavenly Father is perfect. He makes His Word real in our lives through everyday experiences.

> For we do not have a high priest who is unable to sympathize with our weaknesses, but we have one who has been tempted in every way, just as we are — yet was without sin. Let us then approach the throne of grace with confidence, so that we may receive mercy and find grace to help us in our time of need (Hebrews 4:15-16).

God is waiting to help us, but the problem with most of us is that we forget to come and ask for help when we need it. "You can't," my friend Ruth reminded me one day, "and God never said you could. He can, and He says He always will."

Your Greatest Ministry

If I fail as a mother, I might as well throw in the towel with everything else I do, since none of it will feel very important anymore. Our children are our first mission field, and these days a very needy one.

My two teenaged sons play indoor lacrosse once a week during the winter months. Recently, a few of their friends "dropped in" for dinner before the game, something of a custom now which I greatly enjoy and plan for. The two boys in the group who live in motherless homes often wander into my kitchen while I'm fixing dinner "just to talk." They are full of bright conversation and little compliments. "You must really like to cook, Mrs. Kidder. Next time you're baking pizza dough, could I help you knead it?" What they really want is just some time with a Mom. I'm praying and waiting for the day when they will trust me with a real conversation.

My friend Judie seems to always have a houseful. "It's often the little things that keep them coming," she adds, "like a warm welcome, pizza, cookies, fun — not a perfectly immaculate house or gourmet meals." In fact, you have to swallow your pride once in awhile when kids walk in and find laundry all over the upstairs hall, or you looking a wreck. I guess it's those moments that make others feel really at home.

The most indelible impression you or I will ever leave on this earth will be on our children's lives, and yes, perhaps even their friends' lives. The generational impact of your life means that you will continue making a statement through your children and grandchildren to a world yet unborn. If that doesn't make your job feel important, I don't know what will.

The real truth about mothering is that it is the hardest job you will ever do and you are probably less prepared for it than you were for your learner's permit. It is also the most costly investment you will ever make, for it involves giving yourself lavishly for others, filling in the deep wells of self-centeredness in your life with acts of kindness, care, maintenance, and love. You will arrive, as every other mother before you has, at the very end of your own adequacy and strength. When you find yourself like a small child again, needing your Heavenly Father every moment, even as you are needed by your children, you will be exactly where He wants you.

TWO

THE TEACHER YOU NEVER FORGET

Dear Jesus, help me be a good girl and do what Mommy and Daddy say."

The pastor had been preaching on faith and obedience, and as each person searched his heart for areas needing change, from behind me I heard a tiny voice lifted in prayer. I felt a lump in my throat as I thought back to the early prayers of my own children.

An older voice, just as soft, prayed next, "Dear Jesus, thank You for loving us. Help Catherine to know just how much You love her too."

After the final hymn, I turned to greet them. A sandy-haired mother several months pregnant smiled and introduced me to her three-year-old daughter, Catherine, her Norwegian husband, and his very attractive mother, Olga. By this time, Catherine was in her grandmother's arms, with her head on her shoulder and chubby arms about her neck. I was struck by the picture of three generations, wrapped in one abiding faith in Jesus Christ.

What a priceless heritage is passed on when faith is both taught and caught. It is what Edith Schaeffer referred to in her book, *What Is a Family?* when she talked about the passing of the baton.[1] The critical moment in a relay race is when the baton changes hands and the next runner takes off. At this moment the race is either won or lost. The same is true in passing on our faith. The critical moment comes when the child chooses to make his parents' faith in Christ his own. But this decision follows years of observing his parents as they live out their faith.

The Apostle Paul wrote to Timothy, "I have been reminded of your sincere faith, which first lived in your grandmother Lois and in your mother Eunice and, I am persuaded, now lives in you also" (2 Timothy 1:5). It challenges me to imagine what went on in that home. The influence of Timothy's mother and grandmother spills richly down the centuries to us. What glory to God faithful mothering brings!

"I Remember Mama"
Years ago, our family used to gather each week around our small nine-inch black-and-white TV set to watch *I Remember Mama*. How we loved that show! I still remember the children, Nels and Dagmar, and, of course, Papa. But most of all, there was Mama. Her wit and wisdom tied the show together. There was music in her voice, energy in her step, love and honesty in every encounter. But, oh, could she be intimidating! If you crossed the line, Mama became a determined foe, but still the first one you'd run to for solace or advice.

Do you wonder what your children will remember about you? We all pray that they will forget some things, or at least generously forgive. Children learn by your walk, not your talk. What are you passing on to the next generation? What am I?

In our family we have a special grandpa. We all get a chuckle from watching him do the dishes. First, he prewashes every dish. Next, he stacks everything in precisely the proper order to be washed, and fills both sides of the double sink with water hot enough to poach an egg. The clean dishes are so hot they air dry in seconds.

19

As the oldest of six children in a Swedish-American family, Grandpa learned perfectly from his mother how to do the dishes. Much like Mama from our favorite TV show, Great-grandma Kidder would stand by the dishpan, watching and coaching, putting anything that wasn't squeaky clean back in the scalding water. There were other things Grandpa learned as well. All six children played musical instruments and gathered regularly around the piano to accompany Great-grandpa Kidder's rich tenor voice in a family hymn sing. The children learned to pray early in life and must have thought that God was Swedish, for they all remember their father's booming voice giving thanks in Swedish at the dinner table. God's Word was a regular part of their conversation and church the center of family activities. Of the six children, one is now in heaven, and the remaining five are faithful, joyful, and hardworking Christians. Great-grandma Kidder's influence lives on in our home today. She has become a standardbearer for excellence, patient endurance, and love.

The Little Ways

In everything a mother does, she is teaching her children. Her little ways will be remembered the most, for they most accurately communicate character and commitment, faith, hope, strength, and love. She is a model to her children of how to embrace the day, respond to circumstances, manage emotions, enjoy both work and play. They will imitate her attitude toward life and will likely become what she believes them to be.

I talked with several older women whose children are now adults, some in full-time Christian service, asking each of them the same two questions. The first question was, "What do you remember most about your mother?" I was surprised to learn that all of these women had Christian mothers. They attributed a feeling of great security to the fact that their mothers were always home in the early

20

years, especially when they came home from school. A number of them had grown up during the Depression when so many families were experiencing hard times. One friend said, "I don't know what I would have done if my mother hadn't been there. I knew she always would be. Mother would make us both tea and we would talk for an hour or more about our day. It was a special time. She was never too busy for me."

Another said, "My mother taught nursery school sometimes just to make ends meet because my father was elderly. But when she was home, she would have pies or applesauce cooling on the kitchen windowsill when we got home. She made everything smell good. Mother also would have parties for our friends, a taffy pull or a special favorite dinner on our birthday, even though we were poor. No one else's mother would do it."

Another unanimous response was the regular sound of their mother's laughter in the home. "Often, when times were heavy," said one woman, "my mother would let out a spontaneous giggle. It just broke the mood and everyone else had to laugh too. She was criticized for not being busier at church while we were growing up, but my mother was always learning from God's Word."

Another woman remembers growing up on a farm during the Depression. Her mother "was very cheerful and laughed a lot. She also managed our home so well with the little bit of money we had that she and Dad were able to retire comfortably from farming. We thought it was a miracle."

My second question was, "What advice to younger mothers would you consider the most critical?" Although some of the responses varied, everyone agreed on the first item:

● Be home! If you are the sole support of your children, find a job that lets you be there when they leave for school and come home.

● Don't discipline your children out of anger or in front

of others. Be in control of yourself before you try to control them.

• Relax. Don't be too hyper over your children's need for breathing room. Let them make a few mistakes and learn on their own sometimes.

• Learn when to keep your mouth shut.

• Take time out regularly to be alone with God, with your husband, and with yourself. Don't neglect your own needs for rest and refreshment of your inner person.

• Have more fun as a mother. Let your children know how much you enjoy them.

• Love their dad.

Although life wasn't easy during the Depression, some great families emerged from those years. In spite of difficulties, laughter was a regular sound around their homes. Is it in yours? Today women feel torn in two directions by the pressure to generate additional income from their own area of training or expertise and at the same time be happy and successful mothers. Often, they are working not in order to pay the rent or put food on the table, but rather to provide luxuries we all could live without—dining out often, buying designer clothes, enjoying expensive vacations, juggling growing consumer debt, and high mortgages. Is it all worth it? More often than not, the mother feels like she's riding two horses that are headed in different directions! And she may wonder why she ever got on either one of them to begin with! If there's an answer for each of us as individuals, it will be found in developing a clearer focus for all of our many activities.

Taking Aim

"If you aim at nothing, you'll hit it every time!" Dr. Bob Long, a visiting missionary doctor from Taiwan, was addressing a Chinese Bible class about time management. I sat and listened with his wife, Judy, as the Chinese interpreter translated Bob's words into beautiful Mandarin.

"Like an archer," he continued, "who shoots aimlessly

in the air, we will never know if we've hit the mark with our lives unless we take careful aim."

As Bob spoke, I looked over my own life, wondering what I was aiming at. With four young children, I had little time for rest or reflection, so I seized the moment to re-evaluate. Since my conversion at age twenty-five, I had wanted to be a missionary. Naturally, I assumed that meant overseas. I already spoke Spanish and it seemed very likely to me that God would want me in South America. But no doors opened and, furthermore, my husband felt strongly that God was leading us toward his profession as an educational psychologist. The more I persuaded and complained, the more God seemed to be on Steve's side, finally adding four children to our family, and moving Steve very clearly into several new jobs. Sometimes I felt frustrated that my responsibilities were holding me back from serving the Lord in ways I only dreamed about . . . until that day in Bob's class.

"What are you aiming at?" God seemed to speak directly to me.

"Well, I guess I'm aiming to please You, Father. I guess that's really all."

"Isn't that enough, Virelle, if you spend your whole life doing what I want and just pleasing Me?"

How could I answer "No"? God had a way of painting me into a corner until nothing but a yes or no would do. Of course, I answered "Yes," but I swallowed hard, wondering what it would mean for me.

"Here, then, Virelle, is your mission field. I want you to raise these children for Me. When you are done, and have pleased Me with your faith and love, then we'll talk about what I want you to do next. How's that?"

Well, that was just fine, even if it lacked the excitement and glamour of overseas missions. Somehow, I hadn't considered my children as my mission field until that day, but since then, the thought has never left me. Day by day I am aware that God is the one I must please with my mothering. He is the one who has given me this task, and will help me do it with faith and delight. He promises to do the same for you.

What are you aiming at? Does being a mother ever conflict with your goals? Do you ever wonder if God might be more pleased if you were doing something a little more "spiritual"? C.S. Lewis once said, "It's no use trying to be more spiritual than God."[2] Please Him mothering the children you have; find delight in your mission field at home by taking careful aim. We can't hit every mark, and some we will miss many times; but if we aim and keep aiming at a few very critical targets as we mother our children, the others will seem less important.

● Aim at loving them. On my kitchen windowsill I have a little block of wood with the words "Make love your aim" painted on it. I made it years ago at a time when I needed to remind myself many times a day what I was aiming at—not a clean house, perfect obedience from my children, or every project done, but loving them first of all every day. We love them by being there. There is no such thing as quality time versus quantity time. We must spend vast amounts of time just being with our children in order to produce those special "quality times" we hear so much about.

Our children need to feel our love with hugs and kisses each day. They need to hear it from us with a clear "I love you" morning and night. Not just little children but big children too need constant reminders of our love. They need to smell it with their favorite treat from the oven now and then. They need to see it in our eyes or facial expression as we listen to their long stories or problems. They need to know they're loved more than ever when they've been wrong and need forgiveness one more time. This kind of loving is beyond our natural limits. It takes daily grace and replenishment. "His mercies are new every morning," says the Prophet Jeremiah. Ours must be also.

● Aim at pleasing God. Your children will hear your

24

words but may not ever remember them. What they will remember most is what they see you do. Are you real or fake? They must know that your love for God is real and unshakable, regardless of your circumstances, and that it is the bedrock of your love for them. They must be certain of your integrity in dealing with them, that no means no and yes means yes. There are no empty promises, no idle threats.

Children need to see their mothers move through a life of faith—daily, prayerfully, joyfully. They will feel your partnership with the Lord and learn to wait on God, trusting Him to act. In order for them to take the baton of faith, they first have to want it. Will they believe that God is real because they've seen Him in you?

● Choose joy. There is health and balance in a joyful home. Love and faith can be duty-bound at times, but joy sets us free to infect everyone in the household. Is laughter heard regularly in your home, or only the stereo? Do your children enjoy the sound of your voice?

Joy comes to us as a gift when we commit our lives, our way, our will to God's pleasure. It is not the absence of difficulties that give us joy, but the presence of God helping us through them. He takes more delight in us than we ever realize. His promise in Zephaniah 3:17 goes beyond our imagination:

> The Lord your God is with you,
> He is mighty to save.
> He will take great delight in you,
> He will quiet you with His love,
> He will rejoice over you with singing.

Taking aim is the first step to mothering. As we bring ourselves in line with God's purposes, we are better able to cooperate with what He is also building into our children's lives. Feeling His partnership gives us courage and strength to go on.

THREE

MOTHERS NEED A MENTOR

At the end of a difficult day, my phone rang. It was an older woman whom I had always respected and admired. Feeling rather bogged down, I took a leap at honesty. In response to her "How are you?" I answered, "Not very good. This was a hard day with my children. I had a million errands to do, and nothing went very well. Ever had a day like that?"

After a long pause, her words landed flatly, "No, actually, I really enjoyed raising my children."

I was speechless, my conscience pointing a cruel finger directly at me, saying, "She's right! You've got to be a lousy mother to complain about your children and how busy you are!"

In the next moment came the quiet reminder of the Lord, "Virelle, don't feel hurt. She's only forgotten." But she had also closed the door on ministering to a friend.

What every mother needs is a mentor, a trusted friend whose example is worth copying. Had I been without a mentor, that lady's response could have proven lethal to my recovery from a tough day. But I did have one, and her example kept me from caving in. Some years earlier God had enriched my life with a friend named Lorraine, a sea-

soned mother of five, now enjoying life once again alone at
home with her husband. Although we are seldom able to
have much time together, I always come away from her
encouraged. Strangely, she tells me she does too. There
are other women about my age who also seek Lorraine's
counsel and loving ear as they raise their children. She
never claims to know the answers to everything, but offers
an understanding heart and a wisdom gained from years of
experience. Such godly wisdom is the result of seeking the
Lord in the hard issues of life and of regularly saturating
herself in God's Word.

If you have a mentor, you have a treasure. But if you
don't, there's an empty space in your life where one
belongs.

Finding a Mentor

The first and best way to find a mentor is to begin to ask
the Lord to send you one. Ask your husband to pray too.
Most older women have been sufficiently humbled by the
parenting process that they will not see themselves as
mentors. They don't realize the great value of their experience, as they have struggled to apply God's Word to their
lives. Great pearls from small irritations grow!

Your pastor or Bible study leader may be helpful to you
in your search. In looking for the mentor God has for you,
here are a few guidelines to consider:

• Look for an older woman with a happy marriage,
whose children seem to be following the Lord and exhibit-
ing Christian character. This should tell you she's learned
the secret of keeping at least one person happy and was
able to communicate both faith and upright living to her
children.

• Does God's Word permeate her attitude? Is she a win-
some witness or does she put people off by being insensitive? Can she listen to others kindly without offering pat
advice, or does she assume to know the answer to their
problems?

- Do you see in her a kind of service to God that doesn't draw attention to itself? Does she include others so that they can learn, or must she be the sole worker?
- Does she make time for others, or is her schedule too tight?
- Be cautious if she seems discontent with those in authority, or complains about the way she's treated. Look for a contented woman with a teachable spirit. One who is still a learner has brought herself under the Lordship of Christ and the authority of His Word.

Titus was serving the church of Crete when he received this advice from the Apostle Paul about building healthy relationships within the church family:

> Likewise, teach the older women to be reverent in the way they live, not to be slanderers or addicted to much wine, but to teach what is good. Then they can train the younger women to love their husbands and children, to be self-controlled and pure, to be busy at home, to be kind, and to be subject to their husbands, so that no one will malign the word of God (Titus 2:3-5).

The burden here is upon older women not to revert to living to please themselves once their children are raised. They are to give themselves to younger women, training them by friendship and example. This ministry of encouragement and teaching should be the natural next step of ministry. But there are so few older women available because their lives are full of other things. They appear and disappear on the landscape like fair weather plantings. At the time when they are best equipped to serve, their energy is being spent elsewhere.

The Woman Who Has Time
I've told you about my mentor and friend, Lorraine, and now I'd like you to meet her because she is the best illus-

tration I know of an older woman teaching the younger.

Not long ago, Lorraine offered to teach flower arranging to anyone who wanted to learn, an opportunity too good to miss. Approaching me in the church narthex with her calendar in hand, she quickly committed herself to a date. No empty promises here.

Since my mother wanted to learn too, I picked her up en route. She hopped in the car with a bag of fresh croissants and the vases we were to bring.

"What about flowers, Lorraine? Shall we stop and buy some?" I had asked earlier.

"Buy flowers in the summertime?" she countered with a little indignation. "I wouldn't dream of it! You just bring your vases and come. I have loads!"

Lorraine's old gabled farm house sits high amidst trees and looks much like it must have long ago. When we pulled up to her kitchen door, her old red setter, Lady, moved only a little to greet us. Lorraine flung open the door with a wide smile and her usual bear hug. "Welcome! You made it! Coffee's ready."

Lorraine's dining room was filled with a quilt on a large, flat frame. Countless shades of blue on a field of white made a dramatic design in the Lone Star pattern.

"Would you like to see my other quilts, Virginia?" Lorraine responded to my mother's sighs of admiration. "They are all my favorites, and I don't believe you've ever been here before." While the coffee perked, we followed Lorraine's quick step and nonstop narrative through the house—first to their bedroom where a potpourri of color, books, memorabilia, and antiques framed the double bed quilt, her first and her favorite. The bedroom was large and cool, and the floors squeaked about the life still in them.

Upstairs through all the bedrooms, whose walls had once contained the bursting activity of five active kids, we moved under the gabled ceiling to admire the quilt on each bed, all of them uniquely patterned and hand-pieced with love.

"Lorraine, how do you find time to do so much? I could never do one of these a year!" I pictured her as I'd so often seen her in the church kitchen, brushing her slightly graying hair from her eyes, working quickly and cheerfully, a little like the captain of a ship, fully in control of the dinner about to be served to hundreds of hungry people in the next room. I knew it would all taste deliciously homemade.

"The Lord's just given me a lot of energy, that's all, and it's up to me to use it wisely. It's a continual matter of prayer for me to know how He wants me to invest my time. When you pray for me, that's one thing you could pray about."

Lorraine and Gary's home is as comfortable as my deerskin slippers, yet elegant at the same time. Year-round, flower arrangements grace the coffee table. English bone china and candles accompany even a soup and sandwich lunch. There's a quiet, restful atmosphere that's made rich by meaningful conversation and occasional outbursts of laughter from the people who so enjoy being there.

"Let's have our coffee now while I tell you a little about flower arranging." Lorraine placed herself on a stool between us and cleared the round oak kitchen table of everything but our coffee and croissants and a small stack of worn books. Moving brightly from depth of vases and length of stems to circular, flat-sided, or curved arrangements, Lorraine gave us a quick overview of flower arranging. Soon coffee cups were cleared away and out on the table she dumped an armful of color—pink and white peonies, deep purple Chinese iris, greens, and a few orange flowers I had never seen before.

"Now, go to it and I'll watch!" Like a mother cat watching her offspring on its first hunt, Lorraine sat and smiled encouragement from her position on the stool, offering scant advice as we clumsily handled the delicate stems.

"Do what looks beautiful to you. It doesn't have to be the same as mine. Trust your own eye."

We were hesitant and awkward at first, but soon began

30

working with a confidence that bordered on hilarity. In about a half hour my mother and I had made more than a mess of Lorraine's kitchen; we had actually made two beautiful arrangements each! For a moment, listening to Lorraine's whoops of praise, I felt like a fifth-grade girl who had just won a contest—a puzzle of delight and disbelief. Another cup of coffee to celebrate learning something new! And the conversation at her table that morning lingers in my mind like the aroma of flowers and coffee, sweet and hearty.

We listened as Lorraine opened herself to us, allowing us entry, exposing struggles and joys, sharing God's working in her life. She had recently experienced the death of a close friend; she was working through the release of her youngest child to full independence; there was nitty-gritty decision-making on the purchase of a new car, and a mulling over assorted ideas for their coming vacation trip. Central to each issue she mentioned was her deep desire to please the Lord in everything. As contemporary as today's *New York Times*, her conversation was permeated with a zeal for God's wisdom and a hearty embrace of life. She is candid, transparent, and full of light.

Whenever I am with Lorraine, I am encouraged, because I am reminded that God is in the business of making originals, one-of-a-kind works of art like her quilts, each person as unique as our flower arrangements, yet all of us made to carry the cherished likeness of His Son in very ordinary vessels. It is the process of God at work that makes them extraordinary.

Jesus too was confined in a body like ours. He had only twenty-four hours a day to handle a life crowded with people and pressures, and yet He demonstrated that it is possible to please God in every way, to invest in His will, and be devoted to the encouragement and spiritual development of others.

I see this today in a woman like Lorraine who has time, rather than time having her. Regularly and prayerfully involved with others, she is available to them as needs arise. Her calendar is full, but never too full for others. Many times she has deliberately cleared a day of other commitments in order to spend time with a small group of younger women, myself included, who just love to be with her. We would drive an hour or so to Stockbridge or Bennington and snorkle around fabric outlets and small shops, never missing the pottery, and finally stop somewhere for a delicious lunch. Those days have been particularly good times to ask questions and get feedback from one another, without the time constraints that often limit conversations. Frequently, someone would expose a deep personal need or a prayer request and their trust would stoke God's love in every heart. The encouragement and incentive to growth that we received from those times have been tremendous.

I remember vividly an afternoon lunch with a close friend at Lorraine's home. I needed to unburden myself about a deep concern for one of my children who was going through a hard adjustment. As I began to share, tears came uncontrollably. I didn't want to cry—I had planned only to ask for prayer. What I hadn't counted on was the strong sense of the Lord's presence at our table and the safety I felt telling them about such a big problem. They both listened quietly; as I slowly regained composure, they bowed their heads and began to pray for me and for my hurting child with such understanding and compassion that it brought a new wave of tears. That day I knew God was at work, turning even extreme difficulties into milestones of growth. He used my faithful, praying friends to help me trust Him and to bring me deep comfort.

A mother without a mentor is walking a lonely road. She needs an older woman who will be her great encouragement, her coach, her confidant.

If you don't have a mentor, pray to find one. If you are older and hear God speaking to you about being someone's mentor, please take time to listen.

FOUR

COACH OF THE HOME TEAM

I am a struggler. I think I knew it early in life because I struggled with lots of things, one of which was organization. During high school, my bedroom always looked like a bomb had hit it, and it wasn't much improved in college. Marriage brought me the unwelcome challenge of being responsible for two people's messes, not just one. My patient husband often lived with the same dishes in the sink for days until we had nothing left to eat from, and I would break down and clean up the kitchen. He was accustomed from childhood to helping at home, and often did the housework for me. Fifteen months after our wedding we entered the overwhelming world of parenting, and my need to get organized became glaringly apparent.

Little by little, I worked at it. By the time our second and third children arrived, I had a semblance of a schedule, and at least had things looking good by mid-afternoon. Just when I thought I had laundry, meals, cleaning, and diapers fairly under control, my oldest child started school.

No one had ever prepared me for the trail of papers that would follow her home each day — artwork, notices of coming events, permission slips for trips, requests for help in the classroom, library books, envelopes for school picture money, art smock requests, sign-ups with deadlines for everything, and on and on! I was swamped! Where would I put it all? Our home was invaded, papers creeping into every corner of the kitchen, library books sneaking into underwear drawers, milk money and school savings books (what a ridiculous idea!) disappearing into thin air! It dawned on me one day that my younger children were also going to enter school, and if I didn't get a system soon, we would all disappear under a sea of papers.

Under Control or Out of Control?

You know your home is out of control if you can identify with any or all of these problems, but there are other symptoms as well. Do you have clean towels, underwear, and socks only once or twice a week? Do you lose the phone bill? Forget dentist appointments? Do your checkbook and car keys have a mind of their own? Are your library books overdue? Look at your children's hair and fingernails. Look at your own. If you see signs of neglect, it's time to bring your home under control. When was the last time you received a compliment on how you looked, or on what you cooked? Are you on time for appointments? For church? Could you consider last-minute entertaining, or is your house in such disarray you'd be mortified if an unexpected guest walked in?

If a manual could be written for mothers, it would have to include executive level management skills, none of which I possessed when I began, but which I have either developed or am working on now. There are times when running a busy household is like trying to nail Jell-O to a tree. The harder you work, the more impossible it seems. But fear not, some measure of success eventually comes to those who keep trying.

Budgeting Time

Some mothers never admit that they can't do it all, and nearly kill themselves trying. These are the mothers who send their sons and daughters off to college never once having changed their own sheets or done a load of wash. When my oldest daughter arrived at her freshman dorm, she had three boys ask if she would do their laundry for them. One girl exclaimed, "You really know how to use *fabric softener?*"

Time and energy are like money. Once you spend them, they're gone. So decide ahead of time what's worth spending them on. In one sense, time and energy are different from money—if you wait long enough to decide, they're gone anyway.

The Proverbs 31 woman has always had a big place in my Christian life. She has moved from being a finger-pointer to a welcome friend. This woman of beautiful character was a marvelous manager because she decided early on what mattered. She decided to invest her energies and abilities to provide for her family and be a blessing to her husband. Look at this description of her:

> She is clothed with strength and dignity;
>> she can laugh at the days to come.
> She speaks with wisdom,
>> and faithful instruction is on her tongue.
> She watches over the affairs of her household
>> and does not eat the bread of idleness.
> Her children arise and call her blessed;
>> her husband also, and he praises her:
> "Many women do noble things,
>> but you surpass them all."
> Charm is deceptive, and beauty is fleeting;
>> but a woman who fears the Lord is to be praised.
> Give her the reward she has earned,
>> and let her works bring her praise at the city gate.
> (Proverbs 31:25-31)

A most significant characteristic of this woman is her investment of time. Joyfully and with great energy, she

35

saddles the hours she's been given and makes them work for her. With purpose, planning, and training, she provides the motion and inspiration for her household.

God has given each of us a different household, with its own challenges, and yet we all have the same number of hours. I believe that God will hold us accountable for how well we've managed what He's given us. Has it been our priority to lovingly care for the needs of our family and to be a blessing to them? Is it our purpose to honor the Lord with practical planning, regularity in daily responsibilities, and in training our children to contribute to the needs of the family?

Trying to translate all of this into my own life brought me to a few simple resolves. I discovered that my lack of organization had another name: sheer laziness. I could postpone forever those tasks that were distasteful to me, like cleaning the refrigerator, ironing, putting pictures in albums, filing papers, or keeping a running list of household needs. I gave myself a swift kick in the pants and made a wonderful discovery at the same time: most of the jobs I hated could be done in minutes, but the longer I waited to do them, the larger they became. Doing a job when it needed doing was actually the easiest of all, and left me absolutely guilt-free! It took years for me to learn this!

How easy to provide an under-bed box for school artwork once it came down from the refrigerator, to establish a family library shelf for all our borrowed books, to bring shot records and important papers into a central file, to keep lots of quarters in a lunch money container.

With teenagers still at home, even writing this book presents a challenge. Every time we need to wait in a doctor's or dentist's office, I bring drafts of chapters. I am learning to find pockets of time for reading a new book, writing cards or letters to friends and family, or planning next week's calendar. If you come to my house, I may not be able to find the stapler, but I can tell you what we're having for dinner, and you can hang your coat in my hall closet without someone's mittens falling on your head. That's progress!

No Free Lunches

At thirteen, my daughter wasn't exactly "given" to doing dishes. She stood at the sink scrubbing a pan, staring dreamily out the window.

"Feeling like Cinderella, Honey?" I asked.

"No," she responded sadly. "Cinderella had a boyfriend." It was a theme that would last a long time. So was dishwashing.

Teaching children to accept responsibility with a good attitude may seem impossible at times, but it's well worth the determined effort. Making their beds, straightening their rooms, running the vacuum cleaner, or washing dishes—these are last on their list of fun things to do. But then, few of us greet the trash with relish.

Good training begins early. Even when children are toddlers, they can learn to help Mommy put toys away. They also learn by watching their parents serve one another and the family. Where work is involved, the atmosphere at home should be positive and cheerful.

It seemed important to my husband and me to train our children to do their work cheerfully, or at least without complaining. To accomplish this we borrowed a system from our friends and mentors, Gordon and Gail MacDonald. I had watched Gail as a mother. She afforded her two children a lot of trust and I was impressed with the way she had taught them to carry quite a lot of responsibility without complaining. They each had regular chores, morning and evening, and Gail recorded in a small notebook each day whether they had done them or not. Griping and complaining brought a ten-cent fine, deducted on allowance day. We brought Gail's system one step further by making a weekly chart that was decorated with their favorite stickers, and then let them record their own progress each night. There were little rewards, usually a special privilege for an extra good week, as well as small fines for jobs avoided or done with a complaining spirit. The best thing about this system was that it completely eliminated parental nagging. The kids became their own referees and often checked on each other.

"I'll bet Virelle's kids are all $200 in debt!" howled my friend, when she found out about our system. True, there were a few times when allowances approached a deficit. But I also remember giving out plenty of rewards. Today I can ask any one of my children to do jobs without risk (usually!) of an argument. They know how to do laundry, clean the house, make a simple meal, and wash windows. Big jobs often carry a monetary reward, but things like raking leaves are considered family responsibilities. Once when I was out of commission for many months with a back injury, the children pretty much ran the house. Being able to count on them meant the world to me.

Children need to know that they are not simply residents or houseguests. Their unique contributions help to make the home what it is.

Be Their Best Encourager

As my children grow into adulthood, my role as a mother is changing. I am becoming less a manager and more and more a coach of the home team. I'd like to be my children's best encourager. Because of their willingness to help, I am released to do that.

One of the most sincere ways to encourage your children is to thank them for the things they do. When they are learning to give of themselves to others, let them know you notice and value their efforts. Service is love with hands and feet. What a wonderful thing when children begin to use their hands and feet for others. Tell them that God accepts their service as a gift to Him, and that He loves a cheerful giver. How important a child will feel to learn that his service is pleasing to God. Our desire to please the

Lord is the first and best evidence to others that He is real.

I have a small watercolor in my home that I love. Steve had it made for me on a business trip to New Orleans many years ago, after the birth of one of our children. In the picture are four little children running excitedly through a field, pointing up in wonder at two sea gulls flying low overhead. Beneath the picture are Jesus' words: "For the person who does what My Father in heaven wants him to do is My brother, My sister, My mother" (Matthew 12:50).

The picture reminds me that God's "forever family" is made up of those who love to do what pleases Him. In their wonder and cheerfulness they share a family likeness with Christ. How wonderful if children learn to take on this likeness in their earliest days.

Mother, is your child "catching" Christ's likeness at home? Can he see it in you? Is your family focused on pleasing God? Does that awareness of giving Him pleasure filter down to daily living?

In addition to thanking your children and demonstrating cheerful service, remember to express your appreciation occasionally with honest words of praise. Add a hug when you tell them:

- "We could never manage this house without you!"
- "You have such a special way of making our guests feel welcome!"
- "I have no one who loves gardening with me like you do!"
- "I never have to ask you to shovel snow. You're always out there early helping Dad!"

And mean it! No flattery! Children can spot hypocrisy lightning fast, but they also recognize sincere praise. We all need it.

Some morning before school, try asking your husband or children, "Is there anything I can do for you today while you're gone?" Watch their facial expressions. Have you ever had anyone ask you that? How would you feel if they did? Pretty special, I think, and mighty well loved.

Schedule Times for Rest

Just as important as giving hugs, expressing thanks and appreciation, is scheduling rest. No one should be expected to be busy all the time. We all need time each day when no one will ask us to work. "All work and no play makes Johnny a dull boy," goes the adage. It also makes him tired and miserable. When I'm under pressure, I have made the mistake of depending on my children too much. The look on their faces when I call them is a clear signal to me that it's time to let them have some rest. Their lives are demanding too. The last thing I want is to cause them to dislike the sound of my voice.

It's helpful to create a time period every day, and especially all day Sunday, when no child is asked to do any work. Barring an emergency, it's free time. We have limited the amount of activity as well as the types of activities our family will do on Sunday, not because we are overly legalistic, but because God designed a day of rest from work and busyness to be part of the package. Rest as a family, or with Christian friends, is rejuvenating. It builds relationships and relaxes our communication. It also builds a reverence for God into the meaning and purpose of life. We work in order to do God's will, and we rest and worship for the same reason.

Bringing Life into Focus

You will help your children grow in wisdom, and share your vision for loving and serving God, by bringing each day into focus with a small portion of Scripture before they leave the house or take up "serious play." As soon as they were old enough to understand it, we turned to Proverbs in the morning. Before that, we wore out a copy of Ken Taylor's *The Bible in Pictures for Little Eyes*.

Taking turns reading aloud from the chapter in Proverbs that corresponds with the day's date, we covered the whole book many times in the years our children were growing up. It's amazing how often God's Word would speak to problems they actually confronted in school. Gradually, it began to seep into their everyday thinking like honey dripping from a honeycomb. This was my time each day to pray with the children and encourage them in the morning before they left for school. In the evening, Steve often led family devotions and always prayed with them at bedtimes.

These regular times of sharing God's Word didn't always keep my children from making mistakes. Rather, it showed them where to turn when they did. They knew that forgiveness and love were available because of Jesus' immeasurable sacrifice for them on the cross. Only the Lord knows how many more serious things could have happened, had not His wisdom, hidden deep within their hearts, kept them from foolish choices. How I thank God that He listens to their thoughts, feels their pain as even a mother cannot, and encompasses them with His presence throughout the day. No mother or father can equal that.

"The promise is for you and your children and for all who are far off—for all whom the Lord our God will call" (Acts 2:39), spoke Peter at Pentecost, the day the church was born. From the very beginning, the great household of God has been made up of families, as the baton of faith is passed from parent to child within the home. May the Lord find faithfulness in the way this generation brings forth the next!

FIVE

TIME OUT!

I drove Marty home after a get-together with a few friends. We exchanged bits of light conversation in the car, nothing very personal. But as she opened the car door, Marty turned to me with tears in her eyes. "This has meant so much to me to be with you. I had such a good time. Please pray for me—I'm really not doing very well. My husband has to travel all the time and he does volunteer work almost every night when he's home. I'm so tired of being left alone with the three children that I feel hurt and resentful about almost everything I do now. It's really beginning to affect my marriage and my enjoyment of being a mother. I just don't know what to do!"

Remembering the loneliness I felt when my husband had to travel a great deal, I could really relate to her. So I listened and promised to pray for her, strongly recommending that she tell her husband exactly how she felt and arrange soon for a regular time each week when she could do something fun, just for herself.

"Fun!" she exclaimed. "I haven't done anything fun in so long I can't remember what it feels like! I'm sure Dick wouldn't understand. He thinks one of us should always be home with the children."

I'm happy to report that Dick *did* understand, and cut way back on his volunteer activities so that Marty could have some time each week to relax by herself and also with him.

What every mother needs is a regular, guilt-free time out! She has a need for rest and peace in her heart that was carefully put there by her Designer. Like the hub of the wheel, this is the center from which tremendous energy is released for the constant march of demands on her life. Most often, this critical place is left untended. Whether this happens out of love or need or duty makes little difference; the effect is the same.

At first, the problem may be obvious to everyone but Mom. Her joy leaves. It's never the Lord who leaves, but the sense of His companionship throughout the day that withers away as business crowds out all personal rest and her quiet time alone with God. "The joy of the Lord is your strength" (Nehemiah 8:10). And when joy leaves, physical and emotional strength are not far behind. We easily become irritable, critical, and complaining in the way we relate to our loved ones. Life seems an endless struggle.

We all know the snowball effect of irritations on a tired mother. Small predicaments loom like huge barriers to the enjoyment of life. Pretty soon we become so preoccupied with the difficulties that the door of our heart opens wider to self-pity and frustration. We hear ourselves pray aloud like the mother hen encircled by her chicks, "O Lord, help me endure all my blessings!"

Each time I think of it I still laugh, remembering my dear friend Lorraine recounting the first day of school after a long summer with four teens at home. She greeted the school bus that morning with a road strewn with flowers from her garden. The driver made no effort to stifle his laughter as the four teens stepped with singular humiliation over the flowers and onto the bus, hissing, "Mother, how *could* you!"

Well, I know exactly how she could, and it brightens my

day that a fantastic mother like Lorraine sighed with relief when they were all out of the house! Some peace and quiet is necessary to sane mothering.

Time Out for Prayer

If Jesus needed time out with His Heavenly Father, His closest disciples, and friends in order to be continually restored, we should expect to need it even more. What enormous arrogance to assume that we can keep going forever, when our Lord could not. Mother burnout is dangerously common, and yearly pushes up the tragic statistics in divorce, child abuse, emotional breakdown, and suicide. Tending the inner person is not selfish. Rather, it is absolutely essential, responsible, and the most loving thing we can do for those around us as well as for ourselves.

"How do you handle stress?" someone asked me, as we discussed a health problem in the family.

"Prayer," was my instant response. I surprised myself, because I didn't even need to think about it. (I might have also answered, "Cry," "Become irritable," or "Run out and buy a bag of cheddar cheese popcorn.")

As I considered it later, my response amazed me. What a reflex it had become to run to God in prayer when my world was caving in. I knew He had given me a special grace for those stressful times—grace that had humbled and changed me.

Regularly in the account of Jesus' life, we find Him both publicly and privately seeking His Father. His prayers with His disciples and friends warmed their love-bonds with Him and opened their understanding of His kingdom. But it was the private prayer time of Jesus that impressed them most. Wasn't His fellowship with His Heavenly Father already perfect? Why then did He need to talk things over with Him? There was no sin to confess and He never lacked wisdom, so what did Jesus and His Father talk about so often and so long?

In Mark 6:46 we read that Jesus "went into the hills to

pray." Jesus needed fellowship with His Father, time to worship and to share the intimacy of joy and sorrow in the safe circle of perfect mutual love. He needed time to restore His place of peace. It was there in the oneness of prayer that He brought the needs of others to His Father. And He has never stopped doing so, for even now in heaven "He always lives to intercede for them" (Hebrews 7:25).

But when can a mother pray alone? Sometimes it seems there isn't time enough in the day. How many nights I remember falling in bed exhausted, only to be up in the night at least once or twice with little ones. Morning came hours before it was supposed to and my achy body felt like it had slept under the bed rather than on top of it. Without fail, at least one or two small people would climb up on the bed, tap me gently on the face and say, "Wake up, Mommy! I'm hungry!" I'd look at the clock and realize I'd slept through my quiet time with the Lord and feel an enormous wave of guilt. How could I walk in fellowship with the Lord that day when I'd already started it wrong? Feeling defeated and cheated out of "MY time with God," irritability followed closely on my heels into the kitchen for those first precious moments my children would have with me that day . . . moments in which they needed to be reassured that I loved them, God loved them, and everything was all right in their world.

I was well into this established pattern of beginning the day either with "My" quiet time or with guilt when I heard a missionary mom relate her struggle with exactly the same problem. It was the same for her in the jungles of New Guinea as it was for me in suburbia. The light finally dawned on her that she could pray, as she lay in bed with children climbing on top of her, to an understanding Lord who loved to have children climb on Him too. She asked Him for love and strength and wisdom, and prayed both for her husband and each child before she ever arose. She was always amazed at the immediate joy and strength God provided in the early hours of the day, as well as in a frequent "surprise" quiet time with Him later on. When I heard this, I felt immediate relief from guilt and a resolve to try it too. I found that God honors our heart's deep desire to be with Him.

Time Out for Christian Friends

If you and I are too busy to develop close Christian friendships, then we are busier than God ever intended us to be. Think of the amount of time Jesus spent with His disciples. Was it only to meet their needs for instruction in the kingdom of God? I doubt it. Being completely man as well as God, Jesus had real needs for fellowship. So do we, unless we are stronger or more spiritual than He. Friends are essential for maintaining emotional balance.

On one occasion, Jesus "took Peter, James and John with Him and led them up a high mountain, where they were all alone. There He was transfigured before them" (Mark 9:2). So often our focus is on what they saw there— Jesus clothed in a glorified body and talking with Moses and Elijah—that we can forget how the disciples felt. Imagine the sense of trust and intimacy, the burning devotion to One who revealed Himself to them so entirely. Are we ever really the same after Jesus reveals Himself to us? Are we ever again casual with friends who have opened to us their inner person, their burdens, needs, and joys? It is an unequaled trust.

To ignore God's design in our emotional makeup is to invite feelings of loneliness and isolation. Jesus placed time spent with His disciples high on His priority list. We too need an inner circle which includes first our husband and a few trusted Christian friends. Please note that only our Christian friends belong in the inner circle. We certainly want to have non-Christian friends also, but they should not be our confidants or counselors. Psalm 1 instructs us clearly to share confidences and seek advice only from those who are also seeking to live for the Lord and His glory.

Time Out for R & R

If the key to being restored spiritually is prayer, and emotionally is time with Christian friends, then the key to being restored physically is rest and recreation. Fun, you say? You don't mean it's biblical to rest and have fun? How can that be?

I once heard Howard Hendricks say that when he got to heaven he expected God would ask, "Why didn't you enjoy life more?" I have often thought He would ask me the same thing, so sometimes I ask myself. Why *don't* I enjoy it more? Why don't you? I think it's because we have been led to believe that rest and recreation are a waste of time. Yet nothing can misrepresent God more than an uptight and humorless Christian. And what family wants to come home to a mother who can't laugh and have fun?

Just recently a friend said to me, "The kind of people I gravitate to are full of fun and very deep at the same time." What a great description of Christian character! Surely the same God who gives deep joy also loves the music of laughter, especially His children's laughter.

Have you, like Marty, forgotten how to have fun? Would you like a few suggestions? Try one of these:

● Trade baby-sitting one day a week with a friend and meet your husband for lunch. Look terrific.

● Learn to swim, or ski, or play tennis, whatever interests you. Find a friend to learn with and make it a priority you never miss.

● Treat yourself to an overnight trip with your husband or a close friend. Do something completely different from your normal schedule; go fishing, mountain climbing, wander through a museum, take a boat ride on a beautiful lake. Eat fun foods at different times than you usually do. Be silly. Remember how?

● Try your hand at a new craft, or take an evening course in conversational French, or Chinese cooking. Broaden your interests. It's easy to become dull.

● Join an aerobics class with a friend or a new neighbor

47

and invite her home for coffee afterward.

● Spend an hour once a week in a hot bubble bath. Turn on some beautiful music, read a good book, do your nails, or just relax and close your eyes. You'll feel like a new woman.

The list is really endless. Use your creativity and don't give up until you've discovered how to have fun again. Once you get to know yourself, you'll discover that you are really a delightful person!

Making Friends with Your Family

There are times when we need to stop being our usual "mother selves" and learn to cultivate real friendships within the family. Our children need a break from seeing us and especially hearing us in our normal role. They need to see Mom having fun, hunting for shells on a beach, playing basketball, planting a garden with them, being a real person apart from being Mother. To do this may require a special setting away from the usual distractions and responsibilities that trigger our "mother noises."

One of the most perfect places to relax as a family, away from the hubbub, is in the great outdoors. About eight years ago, our family "fell into" the ownership of a wilderness camp in the Adirondack Mountains near the High Peaks region. Accessible only by water, and without electricity or running water, going there is always an adventure. The two little buildings, a kitchen and a bunkhouse, are miracles to us, since all the materials had to be boated in. My husband and a friend built the bunkhouse in the middle of black fly season—a week burned in their memories.

This camp is where our family gets restored. We have all gained real appreciation for the awesome grandeur of the creation, the majesty of bald eagles nesting about a mile down the shoreline from our cabin, the snowcapped beauty of White Face Mountain as it towers above the other peaks. There are beavers, coyotes, bears, wild geese, and an occasional loon.

On one particular morning the mist hugged the glasslike waters. Across our small bay, we watched a great blue heron standing for almost an hour on one leg studying the water. Then, stretching his long neck down, he rose with slow and powerful movements of his wings, and flew across the water and out of sight. We watched in a whispered hush, the silence like worship.

Even more valuable and lasting than our appreciation of the earth's beauty has been the growing understanding of one another, having to depend upon the abilities and contribution of each family member in the wilderness, and savoring one another's humor and depth. We have gone to bed at night listening to the *Chronicles of Narnia* on tape as the lantern flickered low, then have prayed together and fallen asleep to a chorus of bullfrogs in the bay. Memories made there are without equal; family friendships are lashed tightly together.

We have found rest for the body, soul, and spirit. God's still waters are a hundred times better than the world's glitsy amusement parks and neon attractions. Try His high mountains and fragrant forests. If you are not an outdoor camper, rent a little cabin with all the conveniences by the water or in the mountains, but without phone or television. You will come home restored.

Planning

Times of restoring our inner person, of tending the place where God designed that peace should reside, do not happen easily. They take careful planning, from the smallest event like a quick picnic in the park to a "mega-event" like the six-week, 9,000-mile cross-country trip our family took in 1982. (Believe me, six weeks in the car will make or break any family. It was the best thing we've ever done with our children, even though Daddy got dysentery the same day we were hit by a motorcycle.)

Ruth Bell Graham once said, "If Satan can't make you bad, he'll make you busy!" He will also try to keep you and

49

your loved ones from being restored physically, emotionally, and spiritually. We cannot ignore the Master's design any more than we can ignore a car's need for an oil change and tune-up. If we do, we'll ruin the engine.

Sit down for a half hour some time today, alone or with your spouse, and reevaluate. How are you doing? If you're not sure, ask your children! They'll tell you honestly. Listen to them and then make regular provision for restoration and renewal. Everyone will be glad you did!

S I X

ELASTIC WALLS

I t was a first-class snow day just before Christmas. No school! Having grown up in a teacher's home, I knew that called for a celebration.

We had just put up the Christmas tree and baked holiday cookies the day before, so by seven o'clock we had all the makings of a party. The children took turns calling a few other neighborhood friends, inviting them to bundle up, find anything they could use for sledding, and meet in the middle of our unplowed street by nine o'clock. It was a scene right out of a Norman Rockwell painting! Children who seldom played together shared a comradery brought on by the surprise snowfall and a welcome invitation to have fun! Around the corner to the sledding hill they went in a clumsy and happy parade, stopping now and then for someone to make an "angel" in the fresh snow.

I soon discovered myself in an empty house. In a moment of divine inspiration, I'm sure, I stoked up the wood stove until the family room felt like a sauna, turned on some Christmas music, and started making enough hot chocolate and cookies for all of Czechoslovakia and Poland, to borrow my mother's favorite exaggeration. In a couple of hours, the troops arrived home from the hill, happy and frozen, noses bright red from the cold. We dried mounds of wet snowsuits in front of the wood stove while the children drank all the hot chocolate, ate every cookie, listened to carols, and played games. It was the most joyful Christmas party I ever remember in our home. It was such a total surprise to the children, a love gift that made that holiday extra special for the giver as well.

I was a young mother then, just beginning to learn something that would echo over and over in the years ahead. When you give your home, your talents, your time and love to those who can never repay you, the Lord accepts it as a gift to Him and returns to you a joy you never looked for. Children are a very needy bunch. They need others who will care for them, reach out to them, open their homes and lives to them, even their pocketbooks at times, without any thought of being repaid or even thanked.

Welcoming Your Child's Friends
When Steve and I were first married, we visited friends for a backyard cookout. Their next door neighbors had a beautiful front yard, but the back yard was nothing but dirt and a few scraggly clumps of grass. Enclosed by a fence was every sort of children's play equipment carefully installed in cement footings for safety. I commented on the contrast, and my friend responded with a smile, "But you should meet their six children! Because they live in a city neighborhood, they have made their yard the best place to be. Everyone wants to play there! I admire the parents for putting up with it. They know where their children are and who they're with all the time. And those kids are just great!"

It was a lesson Steve and I took to heart. We decided that someday when we had children, our yard would be lots of fun. And it has been! We do have grass but no fence. Our gang enjoyed many years with a giraffe-shaped swing set, a tree house and tire swing, and a huge dirt pile for trucks. The eight-foot picnic table finally died last year and Steve has only just recently stopped reseeding spots on the front lawn worn bare from impromptu soccer games. So often before, his efforts to refurbish the lawn would flourish for a short while, then die out. Steve would shrug his shoulders and say, "That's okay. I'm growing kids, not grass!"

The activity is beginning to wane a bit at our house. This year there's been only one broken window from a lacrosse ball. But what memories we have just sitting outside and remembering the laughter, fun, and yes, the tears over bumps and squabbles and even a few stitches. The old log they used as a "balance beam" is now gone. So are the long, hot summer days when I felt like everybody's mother. It was a costly investment at times, but well worth it.

If your yard isn't the best place to be, there's something wrong. If your children would rather spend all day at someone else's house, you'd better find out why. If your teenager isn't regularly inviting friends over, it's time to investigate. What kind of a welcome do they receive from you? Do you worry more about the dirt they bring in than about their needs? Are you willing to "feed the mob" once in a while? Do your children dare ask you? Do you ever offer?

Every mother has a right to say no when it's clearly inconvenient or downright impossible, and children should respect that. But, don't forget your real aim should be to make disciples of your children—and their friends, and the Lord's generosity and kindness should be clearly visible in you.

Making Room To Reach

"Mom, he has nowhere else to go! Could he stay here for a while?"

The words hung in midair, waiting for an answer. Elaine could think of ten quick reasons why he couldn't, yet she was glad her teenage son had a heart that would reach out to a boy who was embroiled in problems with his family and now with the law. It was a tall order to consider bringing Ron into the home. He was sixteen, known to be dishonest, and a drug-user, and she feared his influence on her other children. His family had thrown him out and had even had the locks changed when he left. Not really knowing what to do, she responded, "Honey, I'm not sure we can. Let's ask Dad what he thinks and pray about it together."

Ron was also a lovable kid who had experienced rejection for many years. His parents had divorced, and he wasn't fitting into his mother's life in another state. His father's remarriage left little time for Ron, an all-too-common story. He was needing, but perhaps not deserving, another chance. His family had had enough.

Elaine and her husband, Jim, decided to trust God with their concerns, and opened their home to Ron. It was a huge leap of faith, but they welcomed him warmly, even making him a birthday dinner shortly after his arrival. He promised to stay "clean" while he was there, and they had many long conversations with him regarding their need to trust him. However, Ron's late night walks and his visitors showing up at odd hours caused them to question over and over if they had done the right thing. When a large sum of money was missing from Elaine's purse, Ron, of course, had no idea what happened to it.

It wasn't long before Ron's drug charges landed him in jail. Elaine and Jim posted bond, promising to secure his appearance in court at the proper time. When that time came, they alone stood with Ron for emotional support.

That was one year ago. In a quick succession of events, Ron entered a drug treatment program which included counseling for his father and stepmother to enable them to function as a family once again. He is out now, drug-free for the first time in years, and is rebuilding his life. He needs yet an additional year in high school to make up for time lost, and will be living at home with parents who are willing to try again.

Recently Ron stopped over at Elaine and Jim's house,

greeted them both with a hug, and told them of his progress and plans. He seemed happy and renewed. He had received his second chance, and he came to express his deep appreciation to the whole family. Their home had become a laboratory where Ron could feel God's arms of love and restraint, and could heal. What a joy it must bring our Heavenly Father when we are willing to be a part of His solution in another person's life. In this case it took a mother who was approachable, who had an open spirit to those in need, and who was willing to pray before saying no. Does that describe you?

If taking such a big step frightens you, take heart. God isn't limited by our fears. There are less risky, short-term ways of reaching out too. When our oldest daughter was in her first year of college away from home, she was drafted into a "Student Adoption Program" where a family within the church she attended "adopted" her for the length of her stay at school. In the initial days of adjustment, being invited to dinner with a family meant a lot to her. Our own family has been enriched over the years by a number of college students who have joined us for lots of events. Many of them have kept close ties with us for years. One year we brought a student from the heart of New York City with us into the woods to cut our Christmas tree. It absolutely blew her mind that people really did those things. She came home and helped us set up and decorate the tree.

Another year a Nepali girl joined us for Easter. As she tried to teach me how her mother made chicken curry, we had long talks about the meaning of life, the Bible, and what it means to be a Christian. She is from a country where it is illegal to be a Christian. Reaching out to students from other countries is an enormous blessing to the family, and a great opportunity for friendship evangelism. These students may someday be in leadership positions in their home countries. Contact with a Christian family now could greatly affect the course of their lives and also the way they respond later to world events.

Loving the Little Ones

One of the greatest needs in this country is for quality day care. Particularly for the mother who wants to stay at home with her own children, in-home day care is one of the very best ways to do it. I cannot imagine a ministry closer to God's heart than one that reaches out to little children. My sister-in-law has managed to stay at home to raise her children by caring for at least one or two others at the same time. She has been a blessing to both her husband and family by being at home and supplementing their income, while at the same time providing Christian love and training to a number of other children.

My second daughter, Amy, and I were driving together one afternoon, discussing her college plans to study Early Childhood Education. Amy has had a deep desire to work in child care since she was only ten years old. She was pensive for a long time before she said, "Mom, I guess taking care of children doesn't seem very important to most people. A lot of my friends are going into medicine or engineering or law. When I tell them I want to do day care, they look at me like I'm stupid! It seems like a second-rate career to most people."

"Amy!" I replied, "what could be more important than raising the next generation? Who is better qualified to do it than Christians?" Then I realized Amy was right. In this world, all our values are upside-down. Of course, the world sees career above motherhood, personal fulfillment above marriage, money over integrity, convenience over care, and on and on. If you are a homemaker, you are made to feel second best, almost a freeloader.

Three times in the Gospels the story is told of Jesus and the little children. Just before Jesus took the children in His arms and blessed them, He said, "Let the little children come to Me, and do not hinder them, for the kingdom of God belongs to such as these. I tell you the truth, anyone who will not receive the kingdom of God like a little child will never enter it" (Mark 10:14-15).

You and I are now His arms, lifting the little ones into our laps. It is our voice they hear that tells of His love, our touch that gives His blessing, our disposition that reveals God's character and personhood. If we as Christian mothers are not reaching out to love the world's little ones as God gives us opportunity, then we will have missed a door that's opening more widely every day.

SEVEN

FROM DISCIPLINE TO DISCIPLESHIP

Linus was seated on the floor, blanket by his ear, thumb in his mouth, obviously needing solace. "Why are you so anxious to criticize me?" he asked Lucy.

"I just think I have a knack for seeing other people's faults," she responded.

"What about your own faults?" Linus returned, throwing his arms up in frustration.

"I have a knack for overlooking them."[1]

How like me, I thought. Mothers have a knack for seeing others' faults in sharp focus. We are on the inside track with everyone in the family. We prod, correct, scold, remind, and occasionally praise and encourage. If the truth be known, most of us find it easier to give a list of areas our children "need to work on" than of things they are really great at. Nothing is easier than focusing on faults; it takes an unusual woman to maximize her children's strengths and minimize the rest.

My friend Ruth Camp remembers many years ago when the principal of their school wrote her a note to report that her eighth-grade daughter, Judie, was noisy and boisterous, and didn't settle down to work. Couldn't she please do something with her? Ruth went right to prayer. God let her know, in His own inimitable way, that she didn't have to fear, that her daughter was sensitive to God—which is what really mattered—and was just going through an awkward stage. Ruth wisely decided to wait and not tell Judie about the note, but to pray for her needs more faithfully every day. It's so easy to be a critic, but it takes a special grace to be an encourager.

That was about thirty years ago, and only recently did Ruth ever mention the note to her daughter, Judie, now a treasured friend of mine, who has a beautifully gentle and wise spirit, and is a great blessing to many.

Cooperating with God

When Ruth told me that story, what impressed me most was her decision to cooperate with God and trust His answer to her problem. I think I might have barreled ahead and greeted my daughter as she got off the school bus with MY feelings about receiving a note from the school principal, and had she considered the value of a good reputation, and just what did she intend to do about her loud laughter and behavior in school? That would have quickly squelched any desire she had to confide her problems in me, and I would have lost a ministry to my daughter.

We need to change the focus of our mothering in order to cooperate with what God is doing in our children's lives. Do we seek the same character in them that God seeks? Is our promise to pray for them backed up by our earnest, heartfelt pleading on their behalf? There are times when our children need to literally be carried throughout the day by our prayers.

It's small wonder so many of us are performance-oriented, when the greatest emphasis in most homes is on what you do rather than what you are. How is it in your home? Can you remember the last time you praised your son or daughter for demonstrating a patient spirit toward someone, or for maintaining such an honest relationship with you that they could tell you the truth when they had done something wrong? How about sensitivity to others, faithfulness about doing chores at home, a cheerful spirit, willingness to share the limelight, or taking disappointment well?

Some years ago I was visiting at the home of one of my best friends after the birth of her third child. Her mother was in town taking care of the home and family for her. Now, my friend openly admits she hates housework. Her home has a welcome "lived-in" feel that I have always loved. So, her mother arrived with rubber gloves and lots of cleaning supplies she knew would be put to good use during her stay. She commented to me cheerfully over a cup of coffee, "I realized one day when my daughter was a teenager that she was never going to be neat. All my efforts to make her love cleaning had failed. But I also realized that she was so pure in heart, it didn't seem to matter much. I would choose that over neatness any day." Three cheers for that wise lady! Is it any wonder her daughter loves her so much and thinks of her as a best friend?

Who's Controlling Mom?

Nothing is more frightening to a child than a mother who is out of control. Child abuse is the glaringly obvious evidence of a parent who regularly loses control. But almost as damaging and bewildering to a child is a mother who has no clear moorings, no obvious order to her life. She lives by whim and fancy. She is either in the mood to make dinner, or she is not. She is not consistently good or bad, kind or unkind, home or away. A child never knows what to expect and can never feel definitely one way or the other about his mother. May he invite a friend home? Who knows? Maybe today she'll be in a good mood, but maybe not. It's risky business dealing with Mom, because you never know what she'll be like when you get up in the morning or return home later in the day. It's never very clear what or who controls her.

A child figures out early in life if his mother's character is trustworthy, and that feeling lasts a lifetime. Hers is usually the first deeply imprinted picture of the character of God on his young life. A mother whose life is disordered and inconsistent gives a disturbing message that breeds fear and insecurity in her child.

Imagine a baby waking from a nap. He cries for the one who always comes to him, always greets him with a smile and a warm hug, always provides comfort quickly with a dry diaper and warm nourishing milk. She shows her delight in him with continual affectionate conversation, little songs and games, soft kisses on his fingers and toes. From the moment this baby is born, he is secure, knowing he is thoroughly loved and wanted.

Now replace this pleasant picture with another very common scene. Upon waking, this baby lies very still for a while. Will it be his mother or someone else who comes in? Will he be greeted with a cheerful voice or an angry one, a hug or a slap? He may not be fed right away, or even changed until his diaper is cold and burns. This small baby has learned the feelings of loneliness and frustration early in life, seldom experiencing regular warmth and delight at his mother's touch. He is confused about her love and sometimes seeks comfort from strangers. This is a picture of a baby who has not bonded to the mother. All his life he will struggle with feelings of insecurity, low self-esteem, and will have difficulty trusting people who say they love him. His own character and personal integrity may be marred, for if he can't love and trust people, how can he love and trust God? Only God is able to reach down deep and heal the wounds of a child raised without the loving bond established and renewed daily from the very beginning with his mother.

Reflecting Order and Regularity

A woman who lives under God's loving control reflects the orderliness of the universe in the smallest of daily events. A child who knows his needs will be met by a loving mother feels a strong sense of security. He needs to feel the regularity of kindness in her acts, trust the tone in her voice, and know that her movements about the house will be safely predictable. Certain things in a child's day need to remain as constant as possible: nourishing and tasty meals at approximately the same time every day, regular routines of cleanliness and hygiene, bedtimes that are pleasant and warm and that always end with prayer. I once read, "Prayer is the key to the morning and the lock for the night." This is excellent advice for us all.

From such beginnings a child first learns about the character and love of God, the order in His world, and the way He wants us to live. Love that expresses itself in faithful service is the firm foundation from which all good discipline and discipleship springs. It never moves or changes.

"Train a child in the way he should go, and when he is old he will not turn from it" (Proverbs 22:6) is a promise many parents hang on to tightly. Implicit in its conditions, however, is a mother who is herself being trained to be a godly woman, pleasing God with every ounce of her mothering.

KISS or "Keep It Simple, Stupid!"

These loving words were scribbled on a piece of paper by a missionary wife as her husband went up to the platform to speak about family life on the mission field. She was actually reminding him of one of the most basic rules they had followed raising their family: that is, keep it simple. Make the bounds clear about what's really important, and don't sweat the small stuff. How we clutter up our lives with rules that don't make an ounce worth of difference to anyone but us! Because enforcing them is exhausting and irritating, we need to boil them down to the essentials. In our home that means honesty, obedience, and kindness.

Children need to know clearly what's expected of them. Too often, we expect them to guess because we've never defined what we want. Parents, in turn, should never embarrass their children publicly, scold or discipline in front of others EVER. It is both rude and cruel to do so. It only takes a moment to find a private place to talk firmly to your child or administer discipline. How many times we have all cringed to witness a child or young person being scolded or insulted in front of others, especially their friends. The thoughtless parent is fueling resentment that may prove very costly to their relationship.

"I don't like the tune in your voice," five-year-old Amy announced to me one day. And she was right. What was coming out of my mouth was anything but musical: it was a cacophonous whine. The standards we teach must first apply to us, or we have no right to teach them. Jesus said that it is what comes out of a person's mouth that makes him unclean (Matthew 15:11). Therefore what comes out of my mouth and yours is going to be our first and biggest challenge. Do we punish our children for name-calling and yet do it ourselves, even in jest? This was a temptation in our house where more than a few of us are plagued by a runaway sense of humor. Sometimes I wonder if Dave will ever get over being called "Fingers."

How's your "tune"? Is it ever demeaning or derogatory? Does the language you use when you are alone with your children match the language you use in front of your friends? Many of us have failed in this department.

We need to lift a high standard for what comes out of our mouths—both our own and our children's. There must be limits on what you can and cannot say when you are angry. Children need to see that anger is not a license for cruelty. "I hate you!" must never be tolerated from any-one's mouth or manner.

Strong discipline, like spanking, grounding, or confine-ment in an older child, should be used only for BIG of-fenses, never little ones. Children can quickly learn to ig-nore us when we overreact to all the little things they can do wrong in a day. Dr. Ross Campbell, in his book, *How To Really Love Your Child*, cautions us to save our "big guns" for the big stuff:

63

I would like to insert a very important piece of advice and warning. The more parents use such authoritative techniques as commands, scolding, nagging, or screaming, the less effective they become. It is like the boy who yelled, "Wolf, wolf!" so many times that it lost its effect. If parents normally use pleasant requests, the occasional use of direct commands will be quite effective. . . . Parents, we must save the big salvos for the important situations. We must have reserve ammunition to handle critical situations.[2]

Your children need to learn that Mom makes no idle threats and no empty promises. Mean what you say, and say it kindly. In a climate of Christian love, no child should feel loved less, but rather feel valued more, by his parents' willingness to set limits and mean them.

Listen to Your Children

Structure and discipline are essential in developing a child's character; but if they are not deeply etched with love and trust, what merit do they have? The whole point of discipline, it seems, is to build disciples, to train children to respond in loving obedience to the great love of God. Love is as contagious as the measles, and when Mom is loving, her kindness infects the whole family. It spreads like a fire burning from one member to another.

Love is the great qualifier. If you are not loving, your training and discipline may have a shallow, tinny tone, or worse yet, a heavy-handed harshness.

If you want to be more loving, show it by listening. If you want to be listened to, earn the right by listening actively with both ears and all your heart to your children. This requires different skills for different ages, but the rewards and insights gained are enormous, worth twice the effort it takes.

Cultivating the habit of listening to children takes real creativity. In young children, one of the best ways to learn to listen to them is by playing with them a little each day. Try entering their world as an unhurried guest, allowing your child to control the play. Children express their thoughts so much better when they play. When four-year-old Lauren played with her favorite doll, "Cookie," she voiced some of her feelings about her new baby sister. When she put herself in the "Mommy role" it helped me understand how she viewed me. One day it really shook me up to walk past her bedroom and hear her scolding her doll mercilessly, give her a spanking, and put her firmly in her high chair. I felt like a monster wondering, "Do I act and sound like that? Am I such an unreasonable parent?" Sometimes what you learn is a real eye-opener.

Becoming part of our children's play world helps us to separate normal childish behavior from outright defiance. There's a lot more room for tolerance when we love and understand our children at the level of their own age and experience. How many mothers fall into the trap, especially with their first-born, of expecting a toddler to behave like a seven-year-old?

Listening to teenagers is less physical than playing trucks or dolls, or building with blocks or clay, but requires herculean strength just to keep quiet long enough to really find out what's happening. This can take hours, a whole box of Kleenex and lots of food, and tasks dropped in a moment when the door to communication cracks open. To miss it is costly. The door may not open again for a long while.

Teenagers seldom want your advice. They just want you to listen and love them, even if you don't quite understand. They want to know that Mom will take up their needs in prayer like a warrior, for that is the greatest comfort there is.

Our children need to know that they are loved, no matter how bad they are, how many times they must be corrected, or how often they fail. We hear a lot about unconditional love these days, but not much about the hours in prayer it

65

sometimes takes to give it. Some periods in a child's development can be unexpectedly trying, and absolute unreserved love, along with a continual fountain of forgiveness, are needed to carry you both through to smoother ground. This kind of love is best found on your knees.

My sister-in-law Cindy describes it this way, "Love them so much that no matter what they've done, they will be forgiven. If they grow up knowing this, they will already have a really good example of God's love for them, and it will be easier for them to follow Him."

Blowing It!

Humility always comes the hard way, usually after a steady diet of "crow," which means admitting you've blown it royally. And what mother hasn't?

A close friend of mine tells about one very bad morning in their home. Her four closely spaced children were all at the noisy, boisterous, and argumentative stage at the same time. Since my three youngest are each seventeen months apart, I could relate to her immediately.

The morning began badly, and there was nothing good for breakfast. My friend felt headachy, tired, and grouchy in the summer heat. Before breakfast was even begun, the two boys were fighting and her girls were whining about the kind of cereal they liked and Mom never bought. My friend soon exploded in anger and sent everyone to his room. It was the first of a series of explosions that lasted all morning.

At noon, tired and resentful, she sat down and opened her Bible. Before she had even begun to read, she began weeping out of sorrow, frustration, and guilt. She called all the children down from their rooms, where they had each been sent three times so far. They filed in like sheep and sat down silently.

What they heard was not what they expected. My friend asked each one personally to forgive her for being impatient and unkind, for yelling instead of taking time to listen, and for not asking God for grace and help when she was tired. Instantly, each child blurted out his or her own wrong attitudes and behaviors. Around the table now sat five sinners in need of forgiveness, and as each one prayed aloud, they all came together to the foot of the cross, to Jesus their Saviour and Lord, to receive a cleansed heart and a brand-new beginning.

"I love you, Mom."

"I'm sorry for acting so rotten."

"I'll be nicer now."

"Can we be friends again?"

"Let's go have a picnic!"

"Yes, kids, and I love you all too. Isn't God good to us to help us all love each other His way again?"

Leave your children a rich legacy—the clear memory of a mother who's willing to admit when she's been wrong and to ask their forgiveness and God's. It will be one of the treasures you will pass on to your children and grandchildren.

EIGHT

THE RESISTANT CHILD

If you are the mother of a resistant child, take comfort. You are not alone. Most families have one, sometimes two. I once knew a family who had just one child, a boy about twelve. Friends of theirs told me this boy, as pleasant as he seemed to me, had so worn out his parents in his first few years of life that they decided never to have another one. He took seven years to toilet train, and didn't sleep through the night until he was ten.

The Ultimate Grace-Grower

The resistant child is special in many ways. For one, you never forget raising him. It is permanently embedded in your memory, like carvings in a tree that say "Johnny was here." He is often embedded in the memories of your neighbors, as well as his teachers, scout leaders, camp counselors, and church teachers. No matter how old you live to be, someone will undoubtedly identify you with, "Oh, you're Johnny's mother! I remember him." It happened to me yesterday.

This type of child exerts his personality over all creation and usually leaves folks exhausted and a little bewildered, asking themselves, "How did he get that way?" Well, I can tell them how. God made him that way. It was no mistake, even though it feels like it many times.

The resistant child provides for us in living color a picture of our own strong will that we keep carefully clothed. Lest we forget how much we whine and balk against God, we see a living illustration in this lovable but difficult child, so that we can learn to show mercy and grace, just as God does over and over again to us.

If you are mothering one such as this, you are closer to God's heart than you know, and He to yours. No one totally understands the long upstream process of raising a resistant child quite like our dear Heavenly Father. He's been working with some of us for years.

There are a few similarities in the resistant children I have known.

● They are usually very bright and inquisitive, learning quickly but selectively about what really interests them.

● In their own opinion, they are always right.

● Bent on having their own way, resistant children learn early how to manipulate the adults around them.

● They seldom have "buddies" for long, since friends tire quickly of someone who has to be boss all the time.

● Mealtimes, trips in the car, visits to other people's homes, and bedtimes are usually very stressful.

● They have difficulty playing on teams or in group games because they don't take losing well and often get in arguments or feel hurt about being slighted.

● They need a lot of affection and approval, and constantly are looking to you for your reaction to them.

● Almost never can they forget themselves. This is a real hindrance to them, because when they want to show love, it is difficult for others to believe they really care.

Finding Out Why

It is important to examine the reasons why a child is so resistant. Is it inborn personality? Is there a physical problem?

69

I once knew a very godly mother whose small son was so disobedient he was expelled four times from kindergarten. She was certain she had done a terrible job of mothering, even though her other two children behaved well. Finally, after a few more years of heartbreak and struggle, her son was tested for food allergies and found to be highly allergic to wheat! For years, his mother had been baking her own stone-ground whole wheat bread in order to give her family the absolute best in nutrition! As soon as they adjusted his diet, her son improved immensely. (Not totally, mind you. He still had a strong will, but at least the family could manage him.)

You need to consult your family doctor if you suspect a physical problem. Discovering the cause of your child's irritability or excitability could bring peace and a feeling of cooperation to your home and eliminate years of struggle with a difficult child.

Sometimes a mother really is to blame for a child's bad behavior. Does she send out a very inconsistent message about what is expected, where the line is really drawn? Does she spoil the child by giving in when she can't stand listening to whining any longer, or to avoid confrontation? Is she home enough, and when she is, does the child ever have her full, undivided attention? Possibly she is making an issue over things that really don't matter very much.

Hanging Tough

Once we decide which rules matter and which don't, we need to communicate the important ones to our children so they clearly understand our thinking. Children shouldn't have to guess what parents' standards are. These standards should be clearly taught, integrated into the whole fabric of life, and practiced by us. We are a living "show-and-tell" of what we teach. We can then be merciful with our children when they fail, realizing how often we do too.

The resistant child, however, will seldom accept our rules without a challenge. By nature, he sees rules as cumbersome, interfering with his freedom and enjoyment. Rather than regarding them as a fence of protection around him, he views all limits as preventing his growth. "Why can't I, Mom?" "I'm going to anyway!" or "Don't worry, I'll be fine!" are his standard responses to the boundaries you set. Herein lies the exhausting part. It has been given to mothers to do the enforcing most of the time. Fathers are a wonderful final authority, but they are seldom there when the child pushes his toe across the line and says, "Stop me!" It is this continual testing that makes the resistant child different. Most children will test the limits now and then; the resistant child does it as a way of life.

Equally as important as outlining guidelines for good behavior is laying down the consequences of bad behavior. It helps if we agree ahead of time with spouse, pastor, or family counselor exactly how we will handle the most common problems of disobedience with a resistant child. Once they are decided, and the child also understands, then half the problem for the mother is solved. There's no deciding what to do when the crisis occurs. Anger doesn't need to surface because we know exactly how to handle the problem.

Let me give you an example. A friend of mine had some beautiful leather chairs in her living room that were a wedding gift from her parents. She also had a four-year-old son who liked to try to poke holes in the furniture with any sharp object he could find. Billy was bright and cute, but always into trouble. (He once convinced my three-year-old daughter to let him do a body painting on her!)

One day when I was in their home, I discovered that Billy couldn't sit on a chair. His mother had told him ahead of time that if he persisted in trying to destroy the furniture, he wouldn't be allowed to use it for two whole weeks. He could sit on the floor, and could eat standing up. Billy didn't believe she'd really do it, but she did, and without any yelling or screaming at all. Billy never damaged the furniture again.

It's important to avoid situations that can suddenly explode into problems, by anticipating them ahead of time. If your child constantly balks at being told what to wear, give him a choice between two outfits. Just knowing that he still has the power to choose may reduce the feeling of being "pushed" into things he doesn't want to do. Whenever possible, let him make decisions for himself. Encourage him to be responsible for the choices he makes, whenever this is reasonable. Avoid power struggles by transferring as many decisions as you see fit to the child and then holding firm on those you know you still should make.

For example, your ten-year-old daughter might be ready to choose her own clothes. Why not accompany her to the store and decide ahead of time the types of clothes that are acceptable to both of you, as well as the price range. Plan for the possibility that you may find yourselves in disagreement in the store, and agree to take a day to think it over. Sometimes, when you're away from a situation, even a resistant child becomes a lot more reasonable.

Each developmental stage resistant children enter presents new challenges that almost always involve privileges. Mom and Dad seem so slow to allow them to do "what everybody's doing." Again, it helps to be prepared. When I found out "everyone" in the sixth grade was allowed to attend a certain teen nightspot run by a local church, I was very skeptical. My daughter felt she had the most old-fashioned mother in our town. I called the school and learned that all the children had been invited to attend over the loud speaker! A local priest had worked hard to organize a teen recreation center where kids could have safe, drug-free fun. The idea sounded great, but we still felt the atmosphere left something to be desired. While our daughter thought she would die of embarrassment, my husband visited the center in full swing, and found it closely resembled an adult nightclub in many ways. There was plenty of supervision, and identification was required at the door. But something smelled fishy. We did let our daughter attend after she begged us to let her go with some friends, but after a couple of times we told her it just didn't seem like the right place for her. Later we learned that some teenagers were arrested for bringing drugs into the center and it was closed.

Had we better anticipated her needs to have fun once in a while with both boys and girls, we might have planned ahead to help organize a junior high youth group at our church. Some wonderful college students did, in fact, volunteer to do that and provided some of the healthiest, most outrageous fun those kids ever enjoyed.

Loving Till It Hurts

Resistant children may be more fragile emotionally than they seem. Regardless of how often they tell you they're right, they know that's not really true. Their assessment of themselves can be a lot more harsh than yours would ever be. A conversion experience for such children is usually profound, and permeates their whole attitude. The strength once used to resist authority now becomes strength of character and a firm commitment to the Lord. That's worth waiting and praying for. While you're waiting and praying, keep in mind these few things:

● Accept your resistant child with the personality God gave him or her. That you cannot change, and He wouldn't want you to.

● Aim to conform the will without breaking the spirit, a delicate task.

● Be your child's advocate when no one else will. Resistant children are often lonely and have a hard time making and keeping friends. When friends leave, it's unbearable if Mother gives up on you too.

● Remind your child often that you love him, and that God loves him. He has wonderful plans for us and never gives up on us.

● Resistant children need grace extended to them more often than others. Grace means love that is freely given, but certainly not deserved. I know a mother who cleaned her daughter's messy room while she was at school, after continual reminders to her to clean it. At moments like those, remind them that God loves us and does kind things for us all the time that we don't deserve either.

• Mothers of a resistant child should take real comfort in this verse: "Those who sow in tears will reap with songs of joy. He who goes out weeping, carrying seed to sow, will return with songs of joy, carrying sheaves with him" (Psalm 126:5-6).

Raising a resistant child carries with it times of broken-heartedness that you seldom experience with other children. These are situations when you need tremendous prayer support. Assemble a team of four or five trusted and mature Christian friends who will pray daily for your child's needs. Be very careful not to break your child's confidences when you share prayer needs. Your child needs to trust you implicitly. Friends who will pray faithfully will make an eternal difference in your child's life.

A small group of older women in western New York decided to get together one evening for special prayer for a teenage girl from their church who had finally left home, after a year or two of open rebellion. She had hitchhiked to the West Coast with a truck driver. They had no idea where she was now, but they did know her life was headed down the drain. They met and prayed for her all evening. That night at eleven o'clock she reached the end of her rope, and called home to say, "I'm coming back, Mom, if you'll have me." This young woman returned home, found the Lord Jesus as her personal Savior, and is now, thirty years later, a pastor's wife. She set a wonderful example for me as a new believer.

God has a way of picking up our children by the heart strings and setting even the most resistant of them on His path. Our prayers and tears, our determined faith and His unshakable love bring a harvest beyond measure. Don't lose hope, and never let go of what God has given you.

NINE

WHEN MOM IS ALONE

After moving five times in five years, my family settled in a small town in northern New York State. We knew no one; my father just liked the town and decided to buy a house there.

I remember that day in 1951 when the moving van brought our things. I was six years old, and went about the neighborhood making friends while my eleven-year-old brother, Roger, helped the movers unload the truck. Soon my father had painted the little house red with white trim, built a white fence around it and planted iris and climbing roses. And then he left.

Those were hard years in many ways. My mother resumed a teaching career to support my brother and me. When my father died just before my thirteenth birthday, I had seen him only once or twice during his six-year absence, but I loved him greatly. In those days, a single-parent family was unusual. All but two other children in my class at school had both parents at home. In our present school district, more than sixty percent of the children come from single-parent homes. It is now unusual to have both original parents in the home raising their children.

When I grew up in the postwar years, a family without a

daddy seemed a lot like the wounded veterans we so often saw. They always bore scars—some were without arms or legs, others carried deep emotional wounds.

It was quite obvious to me that our family was crippled too, just like the veterans, and that made life pretty difficult at times, but not impossible. I remember watching out the dining room window as my mother and brother attempted to put up the heavy old storm windows. They weighed a ton, and my mother was terrified of going past the second rung on a stepladder. When Roger was able, he took over all the heavy work for her and I helped somewhat with housekeeping and sewing. Occasionally I was aware that some people felt sorry for us, and I tried to seem all the more independent and cheerful.

A child from a single-parent family will always carry a mark on his or her heart. When I came to Christ at age twenty-five, He healed the deep emotional scar I had kept hidden during those years without my father. I came to understand that while my place in life might not have been the best, it was what God had allowed to prepare me for His service.

Yes, We Are a Family!

Seeing a single-parent family from the inside isn't the whole picture, but it does give a child's-eye view. This is very important to mothers who find themselves in the same position today that my mother was in so many years ago. Two of the biggest factors that helped our family over those twelve rough years were my mother's attitude and the ways our church ministered to our family.

Because my mother was blessed with a stable childhood and two parents who loved each other, she had a good idea how a home should operate and tried hard to pattern ours after this model. A cheerful and single-minded person, Mother seldom complained, but rather looked for ways to keep making life special for us. We knew we were still a real family. Some of the ways she accomplished that were:

● Regularity. My mother chose a lower paying job as a teacher in order to be home when Roger and I were. We all left together for school and returned about the same time. Dinner was simple but delicious, and ready like clockwork every night at five. That's not easy after a demanding day at work. Nor is it easy to teach children to help with routine family jobs when there's no one else to help enforce rules. By some method, she did it.

● Hospitality. I never remember a time when my brother and I were not free to invite a friend to dinner. It didn't matter what we were having, my mother always made our friends feel warmly welcomed. I never heard her say, "Some other time, Honey. I'm too tired."

We often entertained people for dinner. Everyone helped out. My brother acted as host, Mother did the cooking, I set the table and helped serve. It was good training to learn early in life how to use our home to bring joy to others.

● Special events and family traditions. Holidays and birthdays were big events in our home and provided some of my best memories. Every year after the Christmas Eve candlelight service, we held a huge open house that took weeks to decorate and prepare for. I remember feeling good that people loved to come to our home. When I think now of the work involved, I cannot imagine how my mother managed to do it every Christmas Eve.

● The church as family. Although I did not grow up in the same kind of Christian home that we have now, we did attend church and Sunday School regularly, and prayed at meals and bedtime. It would have been very helpful had we been able to pray together as a family about our problems, but we didn't.

The church contributed greatly to our sense of family. Our social life revolved almost entirely around events at church: summer fellowship picnics at Catfish Beach, youth fellowship, church suppers in the winter, singing in the choir, and the Christmas pageant and candlelight service. I grew to love the people in our small church—they were like family to me. Our young pastor became my brother's closest friend during his teenage years and even taught him how to drive. The church gave me a scholarship for a week at camp three summers in a row. It was there that I first felt God's love. Remembering the truth of His love, the feeling of it at camp, kept me believing in God during my high school and college years when I was tempted many times to abandon my very fragile faith. To this day I feel much affection for those members of our small home-town church. They became our extended family. How very empty and lonely we would have been without them!

Relying on God

During the gas crunch in the early 1970s, our family was living in New England and attending a wonderful evangelical church. We had three little ones, all under the age of five. One Sunday after church Steve happened to walk downstairs to the fellowship hall for something, and came across a young mother and her two sons setting out a picnic lunch.

"Would you like to come home with us and eat at our house?" he asked.

"Well, we're really fine right now, thanks," she replied a little shyly, "but do you think we could do that another time? We're here every week."

"What are you doing downstairs here every week?" Steve returned with surprise.

"I live pretty far from here and my car uses too much gas to come back to church for the evening service, so we just stay here all day rather than miss it. We really need the good preaching and the fellowship. My husband left us a while ago, and we need all the spiritual strength we can get."

"Well, if you don't come home with us next week, my wife will be very angry. She wouldn't hear of you three eating here all alone. I'll tell her to expect you." And the following week, Susie and her two sons, ages ten and eleven, came home to spend Sunday afternoon with us. It soon became a family affair, for we spent almost every Sunday together until we moved to New York.

Susie's story bears telling, for she is a woman who relied on God. Her married life began full of shared love and commitment to God. However, while she was working as a nurse to put her husband through seminary, she watched his love for the Lord begin to fade. At his seminary the Bible was less favored than human wisdom, and this concerned her greatly.

Two little boys were born, and they brought Susie a sense of completeness and joy. Life should have been perfect; but as the years went by, loneliness set in, for her husband was away night after night at counseling sessions and youth activities. His absence was deeply affecting their marriage. One day, her worst nightmare happened, as she learned that he had become involved with another woman.

Susie's life dissolved in pain and confusion. Everything she had believed in and worked for collapsed. She decided that if she was to salvage her family she needed first to strengthen her faith. This was about the time that we met.

Over the years, our friendship grew. Susie spent two weeks every year at a large Christian campground in New York where both she and the boys could have a rest and be nurtured spiritually. A Christian friend treated the boys to their camp experience each year. Susie bought a little tent, and they learned to camp together on weekends. After we moved to New York, part of their summer vacation was a few days spent at our house catching up on each others' news. Steve took the boys fishing, and later even taught them both to shave.

It's pretty humbling being a single parent. At one point, Susie had to supplement her part-time earnings with public assistance in order to be home when her children were. The church offered to help with food and bills when there was no other way.

Disciplining the boys was another obstacle. Susie was

gentle and permissive by nature, and the boys were becoming resistant to her authority. By the time her older son was in the sixth grade, she sought help from the associate pastor. He counseled the boys and took over an authority role in their lives. They became accountable to him for a few years and grew to love and respect him very much. When they disobeyed their mother or didn't carry out their responsibilities, they knew they would have to answer to their pastor; once, that even meant bending over for a few well placed whacks. Both boys eventually grew up to become wonderful young men who love the Lord. They are now attending graduate school, and one was recently married.

"They are my miracle story," Susie glows. Her years of relying on God have brought her the rewards of faithfulness: a great relationship with both boys, and the joy of seeing them follow Jesus Christ.

Being Whole Again

If you are a single mother, God wants you to feel whole. In Isaiah 54:5 God promises you His utter faithfulness: "For your Maker is your husband—the Lord Almighty is His name—the Holy One of Israel is your redeemer; He is called the God of all the earth."

God promises Himself to you as protector, provider, redeemer, friend, counselor, and lover of your soul. He will always be there for you, and you can never exhaust His infinite patience and love. You can rely on Him as your captain over the rough waters ahead. As Christ becomes the head of your home, His body, the church, becomes part of your family. Prayerfully, you can turn to the church as needs arise for various forms of help.

• You can turn to the pastor and elders for counseling and wisdom in difficult matters. Your confidences should be completely safe with them, and they should be regularly available to you for prayer and advice.

• The ministry of the deacons is to meet the needs of

the saints. In our church, that means helping financially with people in need, finding apartments and jobs when necessary, providing help for the elderly, transportation to and from church, meals for the sick, and in many varied ways putting hands and feet on our prayers. Turn to the deacons and let your needs be known.

● You can turn to families within the church where Christ is honored by both husband and wife. Your children need to see many healthy models of a Christian home. Look for every opportunity to join in church activities where lots of families are present. Don't always wait for others to invite you. You can invite people to do things too.

● You can seek a ministry. Making your spiritual life the backbone of your family will naturally lead to some form of ministry. God meant us to be givers of ourselves to others. Ask Him for some way, whatever it is, that you and your children can express love and thankfulness to Christ in service. In doing so, your children will learn to be less self-absorbed and more others-centered, which is a healthy attitude for all of us.

Still, being a single mother is a difficult and often thankless job. Lois Mowday, widowed mother of two and author of two books, recently expressed it, "The two biggest things for me were the loneliness and responsibility. My daughters and the people at church helped ease the loneliness, but no one could help me with the tremendous burden of responsibility I felt. I was the bottom line for my family. Whatever we had and whatever we did was dependent on me. I would wake up in the middle of the night feeling the weight of it."

The church often fails single mothers because of attitudes that are perceived as harsh and judgmental. When Lois Mowday was first widowed ten years ago, she was treated as a heroine at her church. However, divorced women and their children often feel ridicule and scorn, regardless of the tragic circumstances they may have endured. As Christians, we need to leave judgment to God and to those in authority within the church, and make our ministry to single parents one of friendship and prayer.

Single mothers rarely have role models who can demonstrate to their children the fatherhood of God, unless other families, and particularly other fathers, relate to them in a caring way. This is difficult to accomplish, as any single mother will tell you, because married couples seldom socialize with singles. Married women shy away from such relationships, fearing their husbands might be attracted to someone else. The answer to that is for the married woman to reach out in friendship, and then to also include the children of the single mother in family times. The children of the single mom will experience the blessing of fitting into a natural family setting. As a child I was very fond of some of my best friends' fathers. When our families would get together, I enjoyed being an extra daughter in their family. I also "loaned" them my mom from time to time!

Because single mothers are raising their families alone, they have the opportunity to teach their children to depend on the Lord at a young age. Children with fathers just naturally depend on them. They look to Daddy to make big problems go away. Children without a Daddy to turn to have a heart hunger for God. The assurance of His answers to their prayers will stay with them a lifetime.

A home led by one godly parent is always in better shape than a home led by two ungodly parents, or two who are pulling in opposite directions. There is a certain peace for a child who knows that his mom is getting her direction from a loving Heavenly Father who can be trusted.

After I came to Christ and found my heart's resting-place in Him, I often pictured myself crawling up into my Heavenly Father's lap and feeling His embrace. I had been looking for my Father God all my life, never realizing that He was seeking me. Tears came to my eyes when I first read Romans 8:15-16: "For you did not receive a spirit that makes you a slave again to fear, but you received the Spirit of sonship. And by Him we cry, 'Abba [Papa], Father.' "

For the child without a father, nothing in this world could mean more than the promise that we are really loved by a Papa in heaven, who wants us to enjoy the security and measureless joy of just being His child.

As with many painful circumstances, inside there is a gift. Mothers attempting to raise their children alone have all the fierce promises of a God of protection and defense for the widows and the fatherless. And children without a father have within them, early and deep, a hunger to know as Father the God who made them. Both single mother and fatherless child can praise Him together.

TEN

MOTHER BURNOUT

I sat on the edge of the bed one night and realized that every muscle in my body ached from exhaustion. My nerves were badly frayed, as my family well knew. It had been another in a long series of marathon days. I couldn't remember when they began, and there certainly appeared to be no end in sight.

We had four active children, as well as a teenaged foreign student living with us, each with his or her own set of problems which I felt compelled to solve. I was driving for five soccer teams involving twelve games and practices a week, for cheerleading and orchestra concerts, not to mention all the track meets, parent conferences, tryouts of different sorts, and our church youth group activities. School and church were fifteen minutes from home, and I was the only driver available.

In addition, I had agreed to complete several projects at church and had even volunteered, in a moment of madness, for a few others. Deadlines loomed ahead of me like henchmen.

It was springtime, the season of the year that held many of our big family celebrations, from birthdays to visits from relatives. My tired mind visualized endless lists of gifts to buy, parties and special meals needing careful planning, and all the baking, shopping, and cleaning that go along with these.

One night, thinking about it all, I sat on the edge of the bed and began to cry. Big rolling sobs shook me like a rag doll and emptied my body of its last resource—sheer grit. For weeks I had begun each day praying, "Lord, just get me through this day." Now I was too tired to speak, but my heart cried out, "O Lord, please, please, give me a rest."

The way God answered that prayer was to give me precisely what I asked for, but not at all in the way I intended. He brought me through every deadline and sports event, every birthday and celebration to the end of the school year. Then, on a sightseeing trip to Stockbridge, Massachusetts, I literally fell flat on my face, injuring two discs in my back. In the ensuing fifteen months, much of it spent in neck traction and a cervical collar, I learned what it means to rest.

I could bend my neck to read only during my daily periods of traction, and then I read only my Bible. How long it had been since God had my undivided attention! It took three months for my mind to settle down quietly and listen to Him. Like Martha, I had been banging pots in the kitchen for so long that I hardly knew how to be still. As these hours of quiet became my private joy, Matthew 11:28-30 spoke directly to my need.

Come to Me, all you who are weary and burdened, and I will give you rest. Take My yoke upon you and learn from Me, for I am gentle and humble in heart, and you will find rest for your souls. For My yoke is easy and My burden is light.

If the burdens the Lord had designed for me were easy, I began to wonder whose heavy load I had been dragging around so long. It certainly wasn't all His! I knew my life needed reordering or I would waste all my energy on things that weren't God's will for me. For the first time I realized that filling every day with busy activities that were not God's will, no matter how good they seemed, was nothing other than sinful. Because I belonged to Christ, my time and energies belonged to Him also. The way I invested them was one measure of my love for Him.

If I was to learn how to evaluate demands on my time in the light of God's Word, I would have to exercise more wisdom in responding to so many urgent "needs."

Christian women have very high expectations for their own performance, making them especially vulnerable to burnout. Just because our activities seem good, "spiritual," or absolutely essential, that doesn't mean they are. God is still in control, and has proven to me more than once that He can clear the deck of every activity. With one broad sweep of His hand, He can bring down the castles I build and remind me that I am simply His child, here to do His will and to love others in His name. That's all that really matters.

The Signs of Burnout

How do you tell the difference between burnout and just plain fatigue? Why is it so important to identify burnout early and do something about it? And when so many women seem to keep going in spite of a maddening schedule, why can't I too?

A mother experiencing burnout is like a pilot whose aircraft begins flashing red lights warning of impending engine failure. To ignore such warnings at 30,000 feet is to invite tragedy. Similarly, a mother who ignores signs such as progressive irritability, fatigue that is not alleviated by sleep, or frequent inability to sleep, tears of frustration over small things, difficulty making decisions, or moments of unreasonable and uncontrolled anger, is on a train about to derail.

A "derailer" is anything that takes you off the track of God's will. In my life, one of the great derailers is *over-*

commitment. No can be the hardest word in the English language, and I seldom say it without a struggle.

Does God cruelly dump more in our laps than we can handle? No, we do it ourselves, by saying yes to things without consulting our Heavenly Father or seeking the advice of His more mature children. I doubt very much that I will ever reach a point of wisdom where I don't need to do these two things when deciding whether or not something should be added to my schedule. I usually ask my husband, because I value his counsel so highly; if you don't have a husband, then seek out a godly woman or a leader in your church. It's not good to be a maverick in God's kingdom. What greater victory for Satan than a barren, burned out Christian, too tired to encourage or disciple anyone?

Almost forty years ago my widowed mother found herself in a terrible predicament. Her teacher's salary ended in June and she faced a summer without any income. With two children to support, she was in urgent need of a job. A neighbor invited her to work nights at a local cannery, something of a comedown for my mom, but then we had no money.

The week she was hired, the cannery was processing green beans. The beans came down a conveyer belt from the second floor, past a long row of women who sorted them from both sides of the belt. It was monotonous work, and my mother, who is prone to giddiness in uncomfortable situations, found the whole setting quite humorous.

On the third night, something happened to the motor on the conveyer belt, and it stopped abruptly. But the river of green beans just kept coming, flowing down in great waves from upstairs. Within minutes there were mountains of green beans everywhere, the workers below struggling helplessly to contain them. My mother began laughing and couldn't stop. She laughed all the way over to her supervisor as she turned in her hairnet. In a few days it was all a bad memory and she found a summer job in a dress shop. But we never forgot Mother's last night at the cannery!

Like the green beans, too much of anything good can bury you. So it is when the many good things in your life take control: hobbies, your career, chauffeuring children, work at church, even meeting your children's needs. There must be a balance and a clear sense of God's will before you throw yourself headlong into anything.

"Come Apart or You'll Come Apart!"

With these words, my friend Gail MacDonald invited me to attend my first ladies retreat sponsored by our church, Grace Chapel in Lexington, Massachusetts. Gordon and Gail had just begun their pastorate three months before our arrival in the area. We were baby Christians needing nourishment and friendship, and they gave us both.

Loading my overnight bag into her car, I looked back at the front door with a wave of guilt. There stood Steve, holding a baby in each arm, with a five-year-old trying to leap onto his back. I knew what his weekend would be like.

During the retreat at a New Hampshire lodge, I sank into real physical rest, ate fantastic meals, made rich friendships that have long impacted my life, and drank in spiritual nourishment like a starving person. Gail was right, I thought on the way home. If you don't come apart like this once in a while, you really *can* come apart. Jesus regularly needed time alone with His disciples for rest and renewal and so do we. Since that weekend, I have seldom missed a ladies retreat. It is tops on my priority list for personal renewal, and it should be on yours. If your church doesn't have one, find another church's retreat that will welcome you. Bring a friend, and go. Then, commit yourself to organizing a retreat next year for all those women in your own church who missed the joy and encouragement you took in.

If a ladies retreat doesn't sound like rest to you, how about a weekend away for relaxation and reflection with two or three friends? The important thing is to find something that renews you.

88

Rx for Burnout

The prescription for curing mother burnout is easy to give, difficult to receive, and requires the cooperation of others to make it effective. It is found in rest, renewal, and re-ordering.

● Rest. Stop everything you are doing, sit down with your husband, or someone who is close to you, and plan for a rest. Hospitalization may be your next alternative if you don't, like the months I spent in neck traction; realize that you cannot put it off any longer.

● Renewal. Get back to God's Word. If you need help doing that, arrange to meet very regularly with a Christian friend or small Bible study group that will encourage you to read your Bible and pray daily.

● Reordering. Comb through the causes of your burn-out. Like tangles in your child's hair, sometimes they can only be identified after carefully undoing the snarl piece by piece, to find only a tiny mat is the cause. When you find the cause or causes, have no mercy. Cut them out of your life completely, or you'll soon be in a mess again. Then, ask God's forgiveness and grace to reorder your priorities.

As you return to normal life again, consider the example you are setting. If someone were copying you, how would they look and sound? Your children are certainly watching you. How will you feel if they become burned out someday just like you? The thought has haunted me too.

I am learning now to set a better example, trying to receive what Jesus gives me as His will. It is difficult, but I'm learning not to fight when it is hard, but just accept. I am also learning to ask Him before I say yes to anything, even writing this book. How empty the hours spent writing if God had not commissioned me first!

Last, and most important, I am learning that God does not give challenges He does not intend to help me meet. I love the story of the father who asked his son to help him carry a very heavy bucket. The child was overwhelmed by the weight and could not possibly carry it until the father put a long stick through the bucket's handle. He gave his much-loved child the longer, lighter end, while he carried most of the real weight himself.

For years I struggled to carry all my burdens alone, trying to keep a good attitude and trust God to make all my hard efforts turn out right. How completely I had missed the point! When Jesus said, "My yoke is easy and My burden is light," it was because He meant to carry the burden right along with us. The stick, like the yoke Jesus spoke of, distributes the load and shares the burden. And God never gives us the short end of the stick! Everything He wants to do in this world could be so easily accomplished without our efforts, but our Heavenly Father who desires the pleasure of our company gives us the shared joy of effective and fruitful work in His kingdom.

If you recognize yourself as one suffering in some measure from burnout, do yourself and your loved ones an act of loving-kindness. Don't go another day without sitting down with them and explaining honestly how you feel. What value will you be to your children, your husband, or yourself when you are no longer able to function? Asking for help now is by far the least selfish course of action. What a wonderful relief you will feel when you are emptied of the prideful notion that you really can do it all! And how pleased your loving Heavenly Father will be when you give yourself completely to Him for rest, renewal, and reordering. May the Lord bless you in the days ahead!

ELEVEN

SMOTHERING

What can Mommy get you for breakfast today?"

"Don't worry about making your bed. I'll do it for you."

"Oh, why do you have to play soccer again this year? You know you always get hurt!"

"That's the wrong way to set the table! I might as well do it myself!"

Are any of these phrases, or similar ones, heard in your home? In your efforts to be a great mother, have you inadvertently become a "smotherer" instead?

A smotherer is a mother who has gone haywire. She's in overdrive most of the time keeping her home and family running flawlessly — no messy beds or toys left about, teeth brushed to perfection, children who eat not a scrap of junk food and never have grass-stained knees. Smothered children enter kindergarten without knowing how to tie their laces, because Mommy always insisted on double-knotting them.

A smotherer seldom tries more than once or twice to teach her children to do a thing. If they don't get it immediately, she assumes they weren't ready and does the job for them. Waiting while her child laboriously signs his own name to a birthday card takes all her willpower after she's already wrapped his gift so attractively. Children who are smothered seldom think of themselves as real people. Why should they? Mother has been ordering for them in restaurants, picking out their clothes, putting on their socks, and answering for them most of the time.

Smothering is a great temptation since it's common knowledge that it takes less time to do everything for your children than to teach them to do things for themselves. But in the long run it may cost you a lot—children who whine and cry over every new task or simply refuse to try anything new. Later on in life, they may bring six weeks of laundry home from college for *you* to do, or worse yet, may even return home from a marriage that didn't work out with two children for *you* to raise.

As long as Mother is willing to take responsibility for everything, why should a child do it? It's a rare child who will volunteer to pick up his dirty clothes, or put away Dad's tools after borrowing them. A good rule of thumb given to me once is this: When your child can do something for himself, you've got to be a fool to do it for him! Kindly refuse to let him depend on you for everything. Instead, let him hear the genuine delight in your voice when you say, "Great job, Honey! I knew you could do it!"

When a mother who felt guilty if she didn't wait on her children hand and foot asked James Dobson why she shouldn't do it, he answered:

> Think about that for a moment. If you never get free from your child by transferring responsibility to him, then he remains hopelessly bound to you, too! You have knotted each other in a paralyzing interdependency which stifles growth and development.[1]

What an awful outcome for our mothering if we raise adults who can never do anything without our help or approval!

"I Can't" or "I Won't"?

"I can't clean up my room! It's too hard! It's hopeless, and besides, I haven't got that much time before I have to be at school for the game. Can you be ready to drive me, Mom, in about fifteen minutes? I've really got to rush!"

Ever heard that familiar excuse for not wanting to do a job? Couple it with a request to be driven somewhere and you're about ready to boil! What can you do? "Everyone else's mother" lets them leave jobs undone. So why are you so fussy?

Have you ever paused to consider if there's really any difference between "I can't" and "I won't"? I know a mother who didn't allow her children even to use the phrase, "I can't." After she had given plenty of instruction about something and allowed adequate time to do it, a whiny "I can't" was out of the question.

Are your children using their outside obligations to place you over a barrel? You can simply state that the car doesn't leave the driveway until the job is done, or at least begun. With younger children, curtailing their bicycles and playtime with friends is usually incentive enough. With teenagers, car keys and plans with friends are great motivators to keep up with responsibilities at home. *Never* take "I can't" for an answer without responding, "Then let's make a firm date when you can and will do it." And don't waffle on it or allow a string of excuses.

Misplaced Devotion

Have you ever been in a setting where you felt uneasy or uncomfortable about the excessive amount of attention or affection a mother was giving her children? It may sound strange to imply that a mother can be too attentive, too affectionate, or too absorbed in her children, but I think it does happen, especially in homes where there is an unhealthy or nonexistent communication between parents. If a wife has given up on her aloof husband, she may pour her devotion in tireless measure upon her children instead.

93

The resulting relationship between mother and child is an unhealthy one that chafes like a too-tight garment.

The word *inordinate* means "excessive," or "beyond normal limits." It need not imply sexual immorality. A mother who is overly affectionate toward a child is usually trying to fill a large empty hole in her own emotional makeup. A woman who has lost hold of her husband's love, or who may not have a husband, could understandably turn to a child in fierce devotion, seeking fulfillment. It is a great burden for a child to be the sole source of his mother's happiness. The child feels doubly guilty each time he lets Mommy down, as though he had kicked her very spirit. His focus of living becomes pleasing Mommy rather than pleasing God, and often leaves roots of bitterness and resentment that will spring up later in life.

If you are feeling a little uncomfortable with this description, then it's time to be honest with yourself, to admit something is wrong in your home, and to find out why. Are you using your children to fill all of your emotional needs? Do you make them feel excessively guilty when you think they have let you down? If there are deep hurts in your life that need healing, they can infect your relationships with your children in an unwholesome, unhealthy way. You need to consult with your pastor or a Christian counselor and seek the emotional healing God intends you to have.

Kids Are Not Counselors

Another common way we smother our children is by leaning on them too much during difficult times, expecting them to think and to respond like adults. In so doing, we are depriving them of a valuable lesson in handling heartbreak and perplexity.

When there is a serious problem in the home, the temptation often is to talk about it all the time. Whether a marriage crisis, critical illness, or grief with a teenager, situations can arise that previously lived only in our worst nightmares. The weight can be so heavy that we naturally turn to our loved ones to help us bear it.

During such times, we cry together and share our deepest burdens. As much as possible, all members of the family should be able to express their feelings and thoughts about the problem, but children should never be cast into the role of family counselors.

Most Christian homes at some point need outside advice, and God has set in place a wonderful support system within the church for such times. He has given us pastors and elders, mature Christian leaders on whose shoulders God has laid the spiritual leadership of the church. It is to these people we must first turn for godly wisdom, prayer, and counsel. They may, in turn, suggest Christian counseling or other professional help for the situation, but in the meantime, we can know they are regularly praying for us. At least one pastor or elder should remain in close touch with the family from the beginning to the end of the crisis.

This means that your children will always have the model before them of their parents dealing with a crushing problem with the aid of the church. They may not remember your earnest talks or your parental words of wisdom, but they will surely remember the way you turned to God with a broken heart and the way He answered. Children then become partners in prayer rather than burden-bearers.

Letting Go, Little by Little

During the writing of this book, I had an experience with one of my own children that reminded me that letting go is one of the hardest lessons I have had to learn in mothering.

One evening my husband and I were both very tired, and wanted to turn in early. Our sixteen-year-old son, Dave, however, was feeling "bummed" (translation: in a lousy mood) over losing his first summer lacrosse game and injuring his finger in the process. He was also feeling like the only sixteen-year-old boy in New York State who didn't have his driver's license yet.

One of his friends came over just to talk, and they both went for a walk about the time I was ready to crawl into bed. I had begun to drift off to sleep when I awoke with a start, realizing David hadn't come home yet. Feeling furious that my plans for an early bedtime were interrupted and panicky about where my son was, I began fussing at Steve about why he hadn't told the boys when to be home, and where were they anyway, and why was he always so "lax" about things? Pretty soon, I had worked myself into a state of angry panic, which may sound like a strange combination, but most mothers of teenagers will know exactly what I mean.

Steve's only comment to me was, "You have to stop mothering him sometime. There's a sixteen-year-old boy out there trying to become a man. Give him some freedom. Give him some time."

I didn't like what I heard, but I gave it some serious thought and prayer. I went to bed and Steve waited up for Dave and his friend. They were home very soon, having gone for a walk to talk and visit a friend.

In the morning I realized that God was trying to teach me something about mothering that I wasn't learning very easily. Letting go little by little means letting go of your child, of course, but it also means letting go of your own way.

When your children are small, you enable them to make small decisions, but still have considerable control over their choices. As they get older that changes, as it should, for there are times when you must step out of the picture almost completely, except for prayer. Your child and God are on the field; you become both spectator and cheerleader.

The next morning I apologized to my husband for my angry reaction to the previous night's events, and went to David in his room to apologize to him too.

"Dave, I'm sorry for being so angry and worried about you last night. I really do trust you a lot, and I know how much you need your freedom and independence to be a man. If you'll be patient with me, I'll make a serious effort to let you have the freedom you need, with a few limits we can both agree upon. I'll also go with you tomorrow to make your road test appointment. How's that?"

He smiled an understanding smile, gave me a little hug and a kiss on the cheek, and said, "That's okay, Mom. I'm sorry I made you worry. Now how soon do you think we could get that appointment?"

God doesn't want us to smother our children with fears about what might happen to them, keeping them from growing up to be independent men and women. He wants us to trust His ability to guide them and keep them from evil.

Recently my friend, Judie, gave me a copy of *Lena* by Margaret Jensen.[2] In it Margaret relates the story of her friendship with Lena, who was housekeeper and cook in the college infirmary where Margaret was nurse. Lena's powerful prayer life and dauntless faith helped Margaret to trust God to lead her own "prodigal son" back to his family and his Lord. I still see Lena in her college kitchen "callin' out the names" to the Lord of every student who poured out their problems to her over a cup of "Lena tea."

Her example has taught me to begin each day praying for my children too, "callin' out their names" like Lena, saying, "Lord, here are my children. You take them today, Lord, and do what seems best to You, not me. Keep them from evil, Lord, and keep them on Your path. They're all Yours, Lord, they're all Yours."

TWELVE

THE ENEMY WITHIN

It was the fifth Saturday in a row that I had washed and ironed Steve's clothes only to pack them again Sunday evening for another week of travel. His new job was stimulating and exciting. He traveled all over the country, met with officials in Washington, D.C., stayed in plush hotels from which he would call to say, "I wish you were here!"

Well, I wished I were there too. While he was buckling up for another flight in the friendly skies, I was white-knuckling it through freeway traffic en route home from the airport with three small children buckled up in the backseat. Sometimes it took me as long to get home as it did for Steve to fly to his destination.

While I was happy for my husband, seeds of resentment were sprouting deep within my heart. I felt lonely at home during the long days of his absence. Many times the children were sick with winter colds or flu, and I was housebound for the entire week. They missed Daddy and were sad each time they said good-bye to him. I was beginning to run out of cheerful one-liners about how quickly he would be home and what we could do to surprise Daddy when he came home.

Feelings of isolation gnawed away at my self-esteem. Some days I wondered if I served any good purpose other than baby-sitter and housekeeper. It was at the end of the fifth week of Steve's travel that I finally sat down and cried, dumping all my tension and hurt in his lap.

God has blessed me with a very special friend in my husband. He listened and really tried to understand. That alone lightened my load. Then we looked at the problem together.

Feelings of loneliness and isolation are common enemies to women who choose to be homemakers, particularly during the years when their children are young. Even if the husbands do not travel, they often work extra hours to help with the family's growing financial needs. Generally the lion's share of responsibilities for home and children falls to Mom. Without regular relief and adult conversation, she can quickly feel trapped by the permanency and frequent monotony of her role.

There are a few "fixtures" you can install in your life during these years which will help immensely. In fact, once you learn to use them, you'll wonder how you ever managed this long without them. You will need to plan prayerfully for each one, but I encourage you to do so. These are the solutions Steve helped me to find the night I dissolved in tears.

● Find a mentor, an older woman who has "been there." She'll listen and understand and best of all, pray. I had an older friend once who stopped in for coffee at least twice a week during the days when I was at home with three little ones and no second car. We had such fun together, laughing over our problems, discussing even deep spiritual matters while I fed the baby. What an encouragement she was to me! Remember, to have a friend, you must be one. God will give opportunities for your friendship to enrich her life too.

● Train a baby-sitter, preferably a Christian, to take care of your children one or two afternoons a week for short periods. A break at the same time every week can give you an island of quiet to go shopping, get your hair done, or visit a friend.

● Simplify your life. Are there things cluttering up your schedule, perhaps graduate study or part-time work, things that could wait a few years until there aren't as many daily demands on your time? Is housecleaning just too much work? Why not try to find a little money in the budget for some outside help, even a teenager in your neighborhood, to lighten the weekly load?

● Get together each week with other young mothers for Bible study and fellowship. Chip in for group baby-sitting, or take turns in each other's homes letting the children play together if they are old enough. A group of young mothers in our church have organized a group called "Pray and Play." They meet each week at a big city park to talk and share prayer requests while their children play in the sandbox or on the swings and climbing toys. Their prayer times have been a tremendous encouragement to them.

● Establish a regular date night with your husband. Even if you just go for a ride and get ice cream, plan for an evening once a week, a date you just don't break, when you will determine to look your best and when you don't talk about the children all the time. Be one another's best friend again. You'll be amazed at the closeness it will bring back into your relationship to have a regular time each week to be a couple.

If you are a single parent, don't neglect your own needs for adult friendships and fun. Set aside one night a week to do something fun with a friend, or attend a Bible study for real encouragement.

One more change occurred in my life after that fifth week of Steve's absence. God and I had a long talk one morning very early. He reminded me once again that He had a perfect plan in allowing this season in my life. Had I missed it during periods of feeling sorry for myself? He was teaching me a new way of loving—one I would be reminded of over and over again in the years that followed. Loving with no strings attached means demonstrating love in service given cheerfully, expecting nothing in return. Steve needed me very much during his adjustment to a new job. Even in a fancy hotel or a crowded meeting room, he too felt loneliness, but he had no choice. God had clearly put us both in this new job and setting for a purpose. Steve needed me now to love him without expecting all of my emotional needs to be met by him. It was going to take grace.

After I understood what God wanted, I began each day asking Him to help me do it. And He did! Steve's continual travel extended to a total of eleven weeks without a break, but the last six weeks were really a joyful time in our marriage. So much of the problem had been in my own resistant attitude to the stresses and difficulties God had allowed in my life. It was still hard at times, but knowing God was allowing me a new opportunity for loving made it much easier.

Fretfulness and Anxiety

If there is a mother who is not prone to worry, she is either dead or senile. All of us storm heaven with our wits as we wrestle with God's dealings with our offspring.

Ruth Bell Graham, wife of evangelist Billy Graham, has long affected my Christian life. Her honesty as wife, mother, and writer has struck a resounding, "Yes!" in me. Among her writings, a book of poems written throughout her life called, *Sitting by My Laughing Fire*, has spoken to me the most. Here she expresses the anxiety we so often feel as mothers:

I think it harder,
Lord, to cast
the cares of those I love
on You,
than to cast mine.

101

We, growing older,
learn at last
that You
are merciful
and kind.
Not one time
have You failed me,
Lord —
why fear that You'll
fail mine?[1]

Raising our children with fretfulness and anxiety creates unnecessary fears in them. Yet, what mother hasn't had a lump in her throat as her child hops on his bike for the first time after the stitches were removed from his last bike accident? Or, how about sending a son or daughter off to college when they've just barely recovered from two months of mononucleosis? I know a missionary mom whose college daughter had to return to the mainland to resume her studies after spending all of Christmas break in bed sick and depressed from exhaustion. It would have been easier for that mother to tear her heart out and stomp on it rather than put her nineteen-year-old daughter on that plane. What faith she expressed to her husband en route home, after her own tears had subsided, "It must be that God is going to provide someone else to mother her for me now. Perhaps someone needs the experience to be gained by loving her for me." And that's exactly what God did.

"Do not fret—it leads only to evil," cautions the psalmist (Psalm 37:8b). Faith, hope, love, and the other fruits of a spirit-controlled life cannot spring from fear. It is difficult for worry and faith to reside side by side in the human heart. If fear is allowed to thrive, like a hardy weed it will surely weaken faith, godliness, prayer, contentment and can even damage mental health.

"Perfect love drives out fear," the Apostle John reminds

us (1 John 4:18). Fear subsides as the love of God fills our vision more and more. As we trust God to lovingly lead our children, we are released to a ministry of prayer. Unencumbered by fear and dread of the future, we can be expectant of all that God is going to do.

Our family has recently come through a long period of adversity that God has certainly allowed. Crushing difficulties have caused us to depend heavily on the prayers of our friends. It has felt often that we were being carried by them, literally lifted up each day by their love. I have learned the hard way that fears unleashed produce fretfulness and anxiety. A hundred times a day, if necessary, we must refuse to listen to fearful thoughts, or we will be defeated every time.

Recently God has given me a wonderful promise to drive out the enemy of fear. It is found in a prayer of Paul for the Ephesian Christians: "Now to Him who is able to do immeasurably more than all we ask or imagine, according to His power that is at work within us, to Him be glory in the church and in Christ Jesus throughout all generations, for ever and ever! Amen" (3:20-21).

I had spent most of my prayer time asking God for my will to be done, and then imagining the worst. Can anxiety be far behind when we pray that way? When we claim God's promises and believe that He will act, He releases us at once to enjoy our faith in Him again. Then we can grasp reality as God's view of our lives, and begin to love in His name.

A Painful Past

Perhaps you suffer from a painful past that returns to haunt and cripple you with grief. Were you raised by a slapper or a screamer? Can you remember any "warm fuzzies" from your own childhood days, or have they been blocked out by the deadness of years spent with a mother who either neglected you or took out her own frustrations over life with angry words and actions toward her children? Perhaps she was whiny or manipulative and used guilt to make you behave. All our mothers, even the best of them, made mistakes, but some were such bad role models that their influence, like mildew, keeps resurfacing in the lives of their children.

There is a video tape in all of us that replays as we raise our own children. That tape reminds us of our mother's words, her facial expressions, the ways she responded to us when we either pleased or disappointed her. You are indeed blessed if that tape brings good memories, because many women still suffer emotional wounds inflicted by their mothers.

A good friend of mine recently confided, "I have no good memories from my childhood. I almost have no memories at all. All those years were so painful for me—the way my parents neglected me and poured out anger especially on my brothers—that I must have blocked it completely from my mind." As a middle-aged mother she is now consciously forgiving her parents. Raising her own family with faith and love, she is turning a whole new generation toward God. She told me recently, "God doesn't let me off the hook of parenting in His image, just because of the mistakes my parents made." Overcoming a painful past has been her most difficult challenge in parenting.

It is a struggle to reverse the effects of our parents' sins. As teenagers, we were so certain we'd NEVER be like that ourselves, and yet, at times we are. Something turns on the tape and we hear our mother's voice. How could it be that the very things we once hated we are inflicting on our own children?

Some women have had not only insensitive mothers but sexually and physically abusive fathers as well! What crushing baggage they carry into the experience of motherhood! How can they ever break through the razor-sharp fence that surrounds their past and not pass on the nightmare to their own children?

104

Defusing the Pain

A state of emergency was recently declared in our town after an abandoned fireworks factory, housing hundreds of volatile fireworks and chemicals, was raided by some youths. Surely they thought the fireworks not harmful when they took them. But the truth was that they were deadly. Even a spark or sudden movement could set them off in an explosion big enough to blow up a house and kill everyone in it. A massive effort to alert the youths and find the fireworks consumed every parent in the town for more than a week until the explosives were recovered and the old factory cleaned out and destroyed.

Much like the deadly fireworks, the unresolved memories of a painful childhood are innocently carried into adult life and enter our homes. But Satan, who is the archenemy of every committed believer and the jail-keeper of others, delights in dragging out the old explosives and using them on us as we attempt to follow Christ. Are we helpless against his cruel attacks? Certainly not! God's Word emphatically tells us,

> In all these things we are more than conquerors through Him who loved us. For I am convinced that neither death nor life, neither angels nor demons, neither the present nor the future, nor any powers, neither height nor depth, nor anything else in all creation, will be able to separate us from the love of God that is in Christ Jesus our Lord (Romans 8:37-39).

God defuses Satan's evil uses of our past by two means—forgiveness and thanksgiving. God's love helps us accept what He permits, as He allows the pain to touch us. We live in a fallen and sinful world and all feel the results of the choices made by ourselves and others. God who allowed His own Son to suffer from the hateful cruelty of sinners also allows us to experience pain and suffering, to learn sacrificial love and forgiveness. When we are able to forgive those who hurt us and to even thank God for allowing the pain, we will find ourselves uniquely prepared for a ministry for which nothing but our own backgrounds could have qualified us. Far more than that, the painful past that has held us in its grip for so long can become a treasured gift from the Lord. For it can prepare us to bring the healing warmth of God's love to others.

THIRTEEN

THE ENEMY WITHOUT

When asked about her greatest desire for her three sons, Janet Lynn Salomon, former figure-skating champion turned full-time wife and mother replied, "To discern good from evil God's way. To know and seek God's purpose for their lives, and to follow it through to the abundance that Jesus has for them."[1]

Janet Lynn had it all—worldwide fame as an athlete, beauty, financial success. By the world's standard, she could ask for nothing more. But she found it a hollow substitute for the real happiness she feels now. "God has shown me through motherhood that my true worth has nothing to do with being successful. My true worth is only in the fact that God made me in His image and that He loves me the way I am."[2]

What better message can we communicate to our children? God loves them just the way they are, and desires only the best for them. Why is it so difficult, then, for such a wonderful message to take root? Because we are fighting a spiritual battle against a spiritual enemy whose design is to undo us. Our children's minds are the battlefield, and mothers are on the front lines.

The words of 1 Peter 5:8 could strike fear in any mother's heart, "Be self-controlled and alert. Your enemy the devil prowls around like a roaring lion looking for someone to devour." How does he seek to devour them? He uses powerful cripplers like low self-esteem, brings them to their knees with peer pressure, lures them to crave instant gratification with a "mall mentality," and then hangs a millstone about the necks of the weakest ones—the millstones of alcohol, premarital sex, and drugs.

In his classic work *Winning the Invisible War*, E.M. Bounds refers to the world with an interesting twist.

> When the world comes in, it comes in many forms. At whatever door and in whatever form it comes, the world is always the devil's servant. It comes in to do his work as his most obedient and faithful slave. When the world comes in, dressed in its most seductive and beautiful garb, the devil has fashioned its clothing and ordered its coming. The world is the devil's heaven.[3]

In the World or Out of It?

Many parents choose isolation as the answer, trying to remove their children from even casual brushes with the world. In so doing, they create Christian hothouse plants who wither when set out in the real world.

A better defense is to equip our children to handle the challenges God's way. We do this precept upon precept, as we live, teach, and demonstrate our commitment to Christ in the home and by our own engagement with the outside world.

We must be intimately and prayerfully involved in our children's struggles, sometimes offering careful judgments, other times providing friendship and loving support. Some situations are so difficult to resolve that we are completely dependent upon God to act on our children's behalf. Jesus knew the battle would be fierce at times, and He prayed for us and for all who would follow Him.

My prayer is not that You take them out of the world but that You protect them from the evil one. They are not of the world, even as I am not of it. Sanctify them by the truth; Your word is truth. . . .

My prayer is not for them alone. I pray also for those who will believe in Me through their message, that all of them may be one, Father, just as You are in Me and I am in You. May they also be in us so that the world may believe that You have sent Me (John 17:15-17, 20-21).

Whatever challenges we face, God knows about them and has already purposed to deliver us. That brings us great comfort and encouragement, no matter how impossible the situation may seem.

Beauty, Bucks, Brains, and Brawn

The Big Four of peer pressure set the standard for popularity and acceptance and exert such strong control that it's a miracle most kids survive. Only a small percentage of young people hold winning cards: beauty, bucks, brains, and brawn. The vast majority leave school each afternoon silently licking the day's wounds. Some never fully recover.

We recently had the pleasure of entertaining a missionary family for a few days. How amazing it was to hear about the exciting challenges they face in their ministry and how God is using them to reach out to nationals. This family loves life and is a joy to be with. And yet, when I asked the father about his life growing up on a farm in upstate New York, he described in detail the emotional pain he faced from seventh grade on in school. He was bright and interested in learning, and was labeled by other students as someone who would never fit in. "I tried so hard to be liked by the popular kids," he said, "but they just never accepted me no matter what I did. It was the most painful period of my life. Every day I got on the bus just praying for survival. It wasn't until I entered a Christian college and met my wife that I finally found happiness."

Dr. Urie Bronfenbrenner, noted authority on child development at Cornell University—and my daughter's favorite professor—claims:

> The junior high years are probably the most critical to the development of a child's mental health. It is during this period of self-doubt that the personality is often assaulted and damaged beyond repair. Consequently, . . . it is not unusual for healthy, happy children to enter junior high school, but then emerge two years later as broken, discouraged teenagers.[4]

All four of my children have experienced this to some degree. It can take years to rebuild a young life wounded by intense peer pressure.

How can you help your children through this difficult period? You need to be sensitive each day to their struggles and feelings, many of which they keep carefully hidden out of shame. If they are in public school, you need to be supportive at every possible opportunity: volunteering in the reading center, chaperoning school trips, helping with class projects. Soon you'll get a clear picture of what your child faces every day—in a jungle you might not want to venture into yourself.

Another way you can help is by simply listening more and talking less, opening the door wide to safe, nonthreatening communication. When you have listened long and hard, and you really understand, be very gentle and cautious about giving advice. Often a better choice is to pray together for wisdom and encouragement. You should intervene directly only in the most urgent and potentially damaging situations and as the Lord clearly leads. In our home there have been a few occasions when that was necessary, but very few.

Make certain that your child feels successful in something, and has a place to shine. You may find yourself paying for tennis lessons, driving to the skating rink three times a week, or standing in the rain and hail watching him play two minutes in a soccer game. Regardless of what it is, help him feel good about his performance in something. One mother recently told me that her son made it through his worst year in school due to the encouragement and praise of his piano teacher. This older woman, as exacting a piano teacher as ever there was, convinced that boy that he was gifted. It kept his self-esteem from going completely under.

The Mall Mentality

A close cousin to the Big Four of peer pressure is mall mentality. I became acquainted with this subtle creature about four years ago when a new and glorious mall opened near our home. It has now assumed the lead role in the community's social life, from children's birthday parties to casual dating, or simply being the place to go when it's too hot, too cold, or too wet to do anything else. The mall has successfully replaced Mom as the chief chef and cookie baker. It has replaced reading with browsing for new clothes, laughter and good conversation with movies and video games, and healthy dating with "just hangin' out." It seems that the worldview of many children has been narrowed to what's on sale at the mall, what's playing at the theater, and who is going to be there tonight.

Lest all this sound too negative, rest assured that I enjoy the mall as well as anybody, but I don't believe it should be the social focus of our lives. In many communities, what you wear is not as important as where you bought it and what name brand it carries. To some young people, *bargain* is an irrelevant word, and they feel distinctly second-class if they shop in major discount stores. The mall mentality has almost taken over the thinking of many young people.

A huge outlet store in our area draws people from three

states, because of the expensive merchandise it sells at reduced prices. On Washington's birthday, this store sponsors a sale so enormous that people even spend the night outside the front door waiting to be first in line the next morning. The media is always there, and shoppers grin at the cameras hoping they will make the six o'clock news.

It never crossed my mind to be one of those shoppers until a relative traveled some distance to our home, hoping to attend the marathon sale. Reluctantly, I took her. We arrived about suppertime when the crowd was thinning, and traipsed from one department to another, from shoes to sweaters to handbags and coats, milling through leftover items. We were in the handbag department, watching an overstuffed woman elbow her way to the counter with ten leather bags, when the impression first struck me how like a pagan temple this place was. I could almost smell incense instead of leather, and hear chanting before an idol, as crowds of people chattered over the material goods before them.

I came home exhausted. Reflecting later on the experience, I vowed never to set foot in that place again. Even our visiting relative found it somewhat unsettling. Truly it was a form of idol worship, for does not the Scripture warn us clearly:

> Set your minds on things above, not on earthly things. . . . Put to death, therefore, whatever belongs to your earthly nature: sexual immorality, impurity, lust, evil desires and greed, which is idolatry. Because of these the wrath of God is coming (Colossians 3:2, 5-6).

Certainly there's nothing wrong with shopping or going to the mall for lunch. Teenagers meeting a group of friends at the mall for pizza can have great fun. But when consumption becomes a mind-set that replaces activities like youth group, sporting events, or other healthy get-togethers, and when eleven- and twelve-year-olds begin hanging out for hours as "mall rats" trying to be teenagers, there is something wrong.

What's the answer? In our family, we've learned that an open-door policy at home promotes good, clean fun that is a lot better than the mall. Opening our refrigerator and our family room to our children and their friends as teenagers is one of the best investments we can make in their happiness and emotional well-being, not to mention our own peace of mind. It's wonderful to know where our children are and who they're with. It's a nightmare not to know.

Make certain your church has an active junior and senior high youth group. If not, start one, or consider letting your children attend a group in another church, providing you agree with their position on important spiritual doctrines. An excellent youth group must have committed leaders, a supportive church budget allowance, and be SUPER fun, even outrageous fun.

No one can reach teenagers for Christ quite as well as other teenagers. We need to be ready to facilitate every effort the youth group makes to provide fun-filled, enriching programs for our young people. This means putting hands and feet on our prayers for them.

A year or so ago, I felt concerned that our senior high Sunday School wasn't building disciples. The teens were disinterested and their spiritual muscles were sagging badly. "Why?" I asked. The answer I got was that the kids were bored. I wondered how the Word of God had suddenly become so tedious to these young Christians. After praying about it, I volunteered to help teach one of the senior high classes, and the Sunday School superintendent nearly fell over! He told me people *never* volunteer to teach teenagers. Well, I did, and never enjoyed teaching more. It was the most demanding class I ever prepared for, so afraid was I of boring them. The penetrating honesty of those young people so amazed me that often I could hardly wait for the next session.

If your young people are bored by poor curriculum or tired teachers, or by a lack of prayer support for those teachers, don't waste any time doing something about it. Lukewarm faith quickly hardens into a pagan mold. It is critical that we love our children and challenge them while they are still with us.

The Millstones—Alcohol, Sex, and Drugs

Alcohol, sex, and drugs are enemies our children face regularly from elementary school on. They are as everyday as homework in all schools, and it's simply naive to think otherwise. Young people are weak and the enticements are strong and seductive.

I used to think our own school system didn't have much of a drug problem until my oldest daughter was in sixth grade and one of the brightest students in the class tried to sell her drugs during English class. A few years later, my second daughter turned in a drug dealer in eighth grade and, as a result, was granted police protection. It astounded me that many children knew the "new girl" was dealing drugs but were afraid to tell a teacher.

Recently, I asked one of my sons if it were true that any type of drug was available at the high school. A little astonished at my ignorance, he replied, "Mom, in ten minutes you can get anything from marijuana to crack."

"How come kids don't turn these creeps in?" I asked, feeling my blood pressure rise. "Think of the lives they ruin!"

"Mom, you don't understand," he answered in a lowered voice. "You're outnumbered. You'll get found under a car in the parking lot. Everyone's afraid of them. They all have connections on the outside." He was right. After talking with a policeman, I realized even more what a risk our daughter had taken a few years earlier.

Satan is winning battle after battle in our children's lives. Like a master salesman, he is much more cunning and aggressive than we imagine. First he knocks the wind out

114

of their self-esteem, which is the easiest of all tasks. He simply uses their friends to do it. Then he lures their minds toward temporary pleasures. That too is easy, with constant input from the media defining happiness as "thin, fit, rich, and sexy, and with every tastebud satisfied." Lastly, he anesthetizes their minds with the desire for immediate gratification from alcohol, sex, and drugs. Unless the Lord's people extend a lifeline to help our young people find the meaning in life that God intends, there is little hope for them.

A Simple Assist

It wasn't long after I completed my training as a lifeguard and water safety instructor that I had to perform my first rescue. How long I had dreaded that day! Learning to swim at age thirty-five was a major accomplishment for me, and lifeguard training was a required course if I wanted to become a swim instructor. But I still felt very inadequate to save someone, and just hoped I would never be called on to do so. And then it happened.

Mary, my star student in the adult swim program where I volunteer each week, stood perched on the edge of the deep end, toes curled in anticipation of her third jump and fifteen-foot swim to the shallow water. As I looked up at her from my position in the deep water, I noticed that she looked tired and her lips were blue.

"One more time, and I pass," she said with a breathless smile, and in she jumped.

I watched her rapidly lose composure as she floundered, trying to level off and begin her swim. "Take it easy now," I coached quietly, "you're doing fine." With that she went down like a lead pipe.

There was no time for fear or debate as I reached underwater and grabbed her arm from behind, holding her tightly as I swam with her to the shallow water. It was the most elementary rescue, one we had learned early on, at that time called a "simple assist."

Mary was embarrassed by her failure as she choked out, "I just don't know what happened to me. I thought I was okay. I guess I'll never be any good."

"Of course you will," I laughed. "We all need a little help once in a while, don't we?"

Later that night I thought more about what had happened. What if I had been too unsure of myself to grab her? It seemed such an easy rescue, hardly worth calling a rescue, and yet we could have had a disaster had I not been trained. How like our life in the world. People around us are floundering without Christ. Our young people are charging off the cliff in droves, and there are so few to rescue them. Is it because we all feel so inadequate to try to save someone? Are any of us trained enough, even in the most elementary ways, to reach out to a lost world and lead them back to safety? It was then that I remembered the words of my life verse:

He lifted me out of the slimy pit,
out of the mud and mire;
He set my feet on a rock
and gave me a firm place to stand.
He put a new song in my mouth,
a hymn of praise to our God.
Many will see and fear
and put their trust in the Lord" (Psalm 40:2-3).

Once I too was drowning in an ocean of sadness and confusion. A young couple, Keith and Ginny Edwards, reached out to me with simple hospitality and amazing patience, as they answered my questions about their faith. Their "simple assist" changed the direction of my life and later my husband's life, as well. Can anyone even measure the effect on our children and grandchildren? I will always be thankful to God for Ginny and Keith's willingness to reach out to me.

Yes, there is an enemy without, but there is an even

greater God within. Are you willing to be His arms reaching out to today's younger generation? Without you, some will surely go under.

FOURTEEN

THE DARK HOUR

s a young wife and mother, I believed a myth—that by doing everything as "right" as I knew how, my children would grow up to be happy, healthy, honest, sensitive, loving, well-adjusted adults with a deep reverence for God. I thought that if Steve and I faithfully brought them up in the "nurture and admonition of the Lord," they might even enter full-time Christian service. That was, in my mind, the great reward for faithful parenting. I expected God to honor all my best efforts, fill in what was lacking, and make everything turn out perfectly.

In one sense, I wasn't far from the truth. God does fill in what is lacking in our parenting. He looks on the thoughts and intentions of the heart, and knows our motives and desires better than we do, whether we sincerely desire to please Him, or are just going through the motions. When we fully commit our parenting to the Lord, giving Him our children, He parents along with us, leading every step of the way.

That's where the truth ends and the myth begins. God does not guarantee that the outcome will meet our expectations. Neither does He guarantee the process to always "go well." At times, in fact, it can go awfully, and God can seem very far away, even as He maintains His perfect sovereignty in our lives. What He does with our children is His business, not ours. The focus of mothering is not to raise wonderful children who meet all our expectations or bring honor and glory to us. The focus of our mothering should be to raise children who please God, who become what He desires, and who bring honor and glory to Him. This objective almost always requires a dark hour in our lives and theirs, a time of testing that strains belief.

Just this morning a friend reminded me that times of severe testings must come, that they are an integral part of God's plan. "Do not be surprised," she quoted from 1 Peter 4:12-13, "at the painful trial you are suffering, as though something strange were happening to you. But rejoice that you participate in the sufferings of Christ, so that you may be overjoyed when His glory is revealed."

"The dark hour" has nothing to do with strenuous difficulties or fatigue. Neither is it dealing with a disruptive or hyperactive child day after day. The dark hour is much, much worse. Suddenly and without remedy, the worst nightmare occurs in a child's life and you realize that all the years you spent protecting, cautioning, planning so carefully for his safety and well-being can't begin to touch this thing.

I have seen mothers and fathers devastated as they watched their children suffer from strokes, cancer, kidney failure, and emotional breakdowns. Just as grievous are the self-inflicted woes: criminal charges for shoplifting, drug and alcohol abuse, pregnancy out of wedlock, anorexia nervosa, and a deep dishonesty evidenced in chronic lying or cheating in school. It would be easier to go through the darkness yourself than to watch your child face the horrible reality at hand.

Your first question is bound to be, "Why did God allow this? He could have prevented it!" Quickly following are the questions, "Where did I go wrong? Is God punishing me for something?" Although God may have allowed the trial in order to help your child make a clean end with some sin, it is doubtful He is punishing you as a parent through your child. God's forgiveness is full and complete.

First Peter 1:7 speaks of trials as a proving ground for faith and mettle. "These have come," Peter reminds us, "so that your faith—of greater worth than gold, which perishes even though refined by fire—may be proved genuine and may result in praise, glory and honor when Jesus Christ is revealed."

If faith is really worth more than gold, then surely the fire that refines your child's faith will indeed be hot. And the darker the hour, the hotter the fire that refines the faith of both parent and child. It is God's way of touching our inner selves with His sovereignty, His holiness, and His redeeming love. As hard as this is, we must not stand in the way of that process, rather, we must allow our child to wrestle with God and meet Him on his own.

When Children Fail

Watching children experience times of intense personal failure is agonizing. In matters of faith and character, this is where the rubber meets the road. Will they make it or not? How much should you help them? With young children, you must be very sensitive to the Holy Spirit whether to intervene on their behalf. On two or three occasions, I regret not intervening for my children. I think I expected too much from them at the time. A few words on their behalf would have been enough to have rectified a needlessly painful situation in the classroom or neighborhood. But in general, Steve and I both have tried to allow them the freedom to handle difficulties by themselves, yet with lots of support from home.

But difficulties with older children whom God has painted into a corner are entirely different. It's important to turn immediately to the Lord in prayer for discernment, so that we do not interfere in His most powerful lessons. Like a test pilot stepping into the cockpit of his aircraft, a young person facing a deep personal trial must go it alone. A mother has to stay behind and wait.

Today's world has no shortage of opportunities for failure, especially for teens. Dating relationships can turn into nightmarish entanglements; team sports and academics alike can deliver harsh messages about personal worth; family problems sometimes reveal the worst in a person's character.

As painful as it is to stand by and watch, we must resist the great temptation to step in and "fix it." Remember that God is in control, and that this trial is completely in His hands. It is He who meets our children on the proving ground. Failure and disappointment are mighty tools in God's hand to shape their will, direct their lives, and fashion their character after His own. And He makes no mistakes.

Giving Them Back

One of Steve's colleagues at work recently learned that his eight-year-old daughter was suffering from an aggressive form of bone cancer. He will never be the same again. The treatment, which probably is worse than the disease, is heartbreaking. How we all are praying for his daughter daily, constantly calling out her name to the Most High, our omnipotent Heavenly Father! If He can fix anything, why not this? It would be so easy for Him to eradicate the cancer in this one precious little life and spare both her and her parents the agony they're going through! Will He answer? Yes, He will. That I'm sure of. But how He will answer, I don't know.

Our children are a temporary trust to us, like a gift we cannot keep, but can rather hold and love for awhile. Times of serious illness or death remind us of the finality of all of life. Why does God require this of us? How do we reconcile God's character with the cruel realities of life? As we watch and wait and grieve, we wrestle with God even more than our children do.

During a period of grieving over the trials of one of my children, I realized through my tears that I had forgotten the grief God Himself has experienced. Somehow, I thought of Him as above all that, as the giver of grief rather than a fellow-sufferer. But I remembered suddenly that He too was a parent not only of all His children on earth, but of one precious Son whom He had given out of love to an ungrateful and sinful world. Who can really cry with you but another parent who has suffered the same way? Who understands the loss of a child, or the pain of rejection quite like another who has been through the same suffering? I knew that God understood my deep sadness and that He wept with me.

Surely God the Father could have prevented His own Son's suffering and cruel death, but He didn't. He could have spared Himself the dark hour, but He didn't. His own love for the world cost Him an intensity of suffering and pain that ours can only approach. As a result, the door to heaven was flung wide open for all who would enter in by way of Jesus' shed blood. How costly the cross—and how necessary!

If a season of fire has come into your home, it will be costly. But it is also necessary to accomplish God's purposes which are deeper than we can ever hope to understand.

When our children are infants, we present them to the Lord, sealing our commitment to raise them to know, love, and obey the Lord the best we possibly can. This is no easy job. But there comes a time when God asks us to fulfill our promise by giving them back. Regardless of how long we've had them, now they must be His totally.

We needn't be surprised by this. The Bible is full of examples we may have thought would never apply to us. But they do. Hannah relinquished Samuel to Eli the priest (1 Samuel 1:28); Moses' mother placed the "fine child" God had given her in a basket in the Nile reeds (Exodus 2:2-3); Elizabeth and Mary gave birth to children they

knew God had ordained for some holy and mysterious purpose right from conception (Luke 1:35-36); Eunice released her son, Timothy, to follow Paul in spreading the
Gospel, she knew not where. As these women gave their
children back to God, they enriched the world. Ruth Bell
Graham expressed the relinquishment this way:

> We live a time
> secure;
> beloved and loving,
> sure
> it cannot last
> for long
> then—
> the goodbyes come
> again—again—
> like a small death,
> the closing of a door.
> One learns to live
> with pain.
> One looks ahead,
> not back—
> never back,
> only before.
> And joy will come again—
> warm and secure,
> if only for the now,
> laughing,
> we endure.[1]

Mothes like this rest their sadness as an offering on the
ashes of their will, letting go of their dear children into the
hands of One who loves them more.

Shared Struggles, Shared Joys

One of the values in our darkest hours is in lifting them up
to identify with another's suffering—not to give answers,

but to love, to understand, and to pray effectively. Those hours of our deepest need become monuments to God's faithfulness and His sustaining grace.

At a recent ladies retreat, my friend Ruth Camp shared her struggle with her son Bob. Seldom have I heard a story that has moved me so, and with her permission, I share it with you.[2]

Bob was the youngest of Ruth's five children, "a husky lad, good-looking, shy, sensitive, a kind boy. He loved animals and babies, the out-of-doors, family and friends. At the age of five, Bob received Jesus Christ into his heart as his Saviour, and in spite of the struggle ahead, he never doubted the validity of that decision."

Bob was a rascal too, and Ruth's nerves were stretched by the constant tumbling and wrestling of her two youngest sons, Steve and Bob. I could relate to that, because I have also raised two boys close in age!

When Bob was fifteen, his dad suddenly collapsed with a massive coronary. He died in the arms of his two teenaged sons. Bob was never the same again. The night after his father's funeral, he went to the home of friends Ruth knew little about. "Why did he have to leave now?" she wondered. "He needs his family—US—at such a difficult time!" Bob seemed to have silently stepped off the path.

As Bob continued a steady involvement with these friends, months turned to years. Before long Ruth knew he was drinking and smoking pot. One of his best friends, a boy named Dan, was the son of one of Ruth's friends. Both women prayed long and hard for their sons, trusting God to turn them around. Without her husband's help and support with Bob, Ruth found the difficulties overwhelming. Like most of us, she lay awake and worried at night, waiting for the sound of his motorcycle entering the driveway. Soon she had three bleeding ulcers.

The turning point for Ruth came one Friday night as Bob was getting ready to leave. She begged him not to go, even pounded her fists on his back in anger and frustration.

"Mom, stop," Bob said gently. "You're only hurting your hands. Can't you trust God for me?"

"How much time have you got, Bob?" Ruth asked, as she regained her composure.

"All the time you need," Bob responded, and together they knelt by the sofa and prayed, mother and prodigal son. In that prayer, Ruth gave her son back to God for the hundredth time. She thanked God for every moment with him, even for the dark times they had shared, and then she gave him back and asked God's protection and blessing for him, that He would hedge him about on every side with His love. Bob kissed her and left.

Ruth told us, "I slept like a baby that night. Bob was in God's hands and under His authority. He was His—he had only been loaned to me. The circumstances remained the same, but the burden was lifted. I was experiencing the truth of Andrew Murray's words when he faced a painful trial.

I was here:
By God's appointment,
In His keeping,
Under His training,
For His time.[3]

A year or so later, Bob visited his sister Elaine and her family in Oregon. In the months previous, he had lived briefly with his sister Judie and her family, and had enjoyed renewed relationships with them, and most of all with his Heavenly Father.

Not long after this, when traveling in California, Bob pulled out onto the highway on his motorcycle late one night, and drove directly into a car without its lights on. He was killed instantly.

When a mother accepts the sovereignty of God in her child's life, she steps with both feet into the river of grace and peace that flow from His throne. Ruth knew Bob was in heaven, and she accepted God's will, bathed in grace.

A few years later Ruth answered a knock at her back door to discover Bob's best friend, Dan, standing there with a yellow rose in his hand. "Mrs. Camp, may I come in?"

"Of course, you may come in!" Ruth whooped in surprise, taking him warmly by the arm and pulling him into her living room. "How are you, Dan? What's been happening in your life?"

Dan began a story that took a long while to tell. His life had taken some wrong turns too, into alcohol and drugs. But a few months earlier, he had come to Christ for complete forgiveness. "I'm trying to start my life over again, Mrs. Camp, but it's hard because I really care about my friends. I know their ways are not good for me now. Will you pray for me? I'm going to need it a lot!"

"O Dan, you bet I'll pray! Nothing in this world could make me happier than hearing you tell me this!"

Later, as Dan stepped down off her porch to go home, Ruth remembered that Bob had already gome "home." Did God decide to answer Dan's mother's prayers for her son by restoring his life, but not answer her prayers for Bob? Had God been unfair?

"Absolutely not!" Ruth declared emphatically at the retreat. She referred us to some words of Hannah Whitehall Smith that she had long treasured: "If our Father permits a trial to come, it must be because the trial is the sweetest and best thing that could happen to us, and we must accept it with thanks from His dear hand." God has a right to every life He redeems.

When Peter was told by Jesus that he would one day die by crucifixion also, he turned and pointed at John, saying, " 'Lord, what about him?' Jesus answered, 'If I want him to remain alive until I return, what is that to you? You must follow Me' " (John 21:21-22).

So often we pray in order to receive good things from God, but in the process of our praying, He is changing us.

The more we pray, the more God helps us to want His will, to bow not just our heads but our hearts. He always answers, and we must believe His answers are best.

As Ruth put it, "God is too good to be unkind, and too wise to make a mistake." When the time comes for you and your child to face your darkest hours, may you find all the grace you need to trust God to do what is best.

FIFTEEN

RELEASING YOUR CHILDREN

One of the hardest things we ever do as mothers is to let go of our children. We shrink back from the kind of test that Ruth Camp faced—committing a child headed on a collision course into God's care. That requires a special working of the Holy Spirit that is impossible to muster up on our own. Releasing is a different process, one that occurs gradually with each passing day.

"It's a cinch by the inch but hard by the yard," said my good friend Peter Letchford. I must have been talking about some great, insurmountable difficulty at the time. (Perhaps it was losing ten pounds!) His words struck home and helped me realize that just about every obstacle can be overcome that way: a little here, a little there, day by day. How good the Lord is to give us time to learn and grow. How gentle He is in dealing with us. And so it is with the exercise of releasing our children to full independence. We do it gently, encouragingly, day by day.

Our responsibilities as mothers do taper off, as indeed they should. Our emotional involvement, our deep commitment of love and prayer will never end, but our daily care giving does. It would be unhealthy any other way. Imagine a mother calling her thirty-year-old son or daughter on the phone to ask if they remembered their dental checkup this year, and were they keeping warm enough on these cold days? I once knew a young mother who dialed her mother long distance every morning to discuss matters that should have been reserved for her husband. The cord between them had never been broken. It is difficult to build a marriage and a home without making a clean break from parental dependency. We never abandon mutual love but emotional dependence must be broken.

When we returned home from depositing our oldest daughter, Lauren, in college, I had a letter waiting for me from a friend at church. About a month earlier, Betty had sensed that I would soon be facing some of the same feelings she went through when her oldest son left home to attend college, and she began composing a letter to me. The letter was so special that I'd like to share it with you. Feel free to substitute your own names for ours!

Dear Virelle,
You might say this is a "Mom to Mom" note. Both you and Steve and, of course, Lauren, are about to embark on a new phase of life—the exercise called releasing. In a way, it's just an extension of what you have been doing with Lauren since she was small. It resembles a physical exercise; at times it hurts. In the long run, exercise is healthy for you. So is releasing.

Remember when Lauren learned to walk? She no longer returned to creeping or holding your hand all the time. But that was okay, right? Then she went to school and wasn't with you all day long. But then that was fine also. On and on throughout her life you have been releasing more and more. You wouldn't want it to be any other way.

You have not lost a daughter. Whenever you release someone or something to the Lord, you never lose, only gain. It's very much the same way you gave yourself to the Lord.

You will only lose if you hold on. (Let's all read that sentence a second time!) In a new way, this new relationship will free you both to respect and love each other in a different dimension. Both you and Lauren will grow. Marilyn Zdenek sums it up nicely:

> It was hard to let you go,
> To watch womanhood reach out and snatch you
> Long before the mothering was done.
> But if God listened to mothers and gave in,
> Would the time for turning loose of daughters
>   ever come?
> It was hard when you went away—
> For how was I to know
> The serendipity of letting go
> And meeting in a new way
> Woman to woman,
> Friend to friend.

Joy in Jesus,

Betty

Friends like Betty, who have "been there" and are willing to encourage others are among life's real treasures.

Betty's advice was well taken. Steve and I tried to allow Lauren to make all her own decisions in college, even when it was really hard. We advised her against joining a sorority, but when she decided to try it anyway, we respected her reasoning. Later, living at the sorority house became a nightmare—her faith was sorely tested there, and it proved too much. A group of Christians on campus began praying about her living situation, and one of them offered Lauren space in her apartment. Lauren decided to move one weekend and called us after she was settled in with her girlfriend. We felt thankful that God had provided a place for her to live peacefully. One of her friends, however, exclaimed loudly, "Your parents trusted you to do that? You moved without telling them and they weren't mad? Wow! I wish my parents trusted me like that! They would have killed me!"

We still have three more children who will soon enter college or career, and our resolve to allow them to make their own decisions will probably be stretched to the breaking point at times. I'm not as naive as I used to be about how difficult this can be. But if we want to raise responsible adults, then we need to allow our grown children the luxury of some mistakes without making them feel like failures afterward. That freedom is very precious to young adults, but it often demands a great leap of faith for their parents.

God Moves In, You Move Out

God prepares both parent and child for separation in unusual ways. Often He uses disappointments and hardships that we would never have chosen to strip away the many distractions in a young person's life until there's nothing left but Jesus.

The final blow for Lauren was mononucleosis, following on the heels of one letdown after another. By May of her senior year in high school, she was so ill that school and final exams were out of the question. For eight weeks she languished at home, fighting the illness and its accompanying depression. After storming heaven with prayers for her return to health, it dawned on me one day that I was fighting against God. He was parenting my child on the inside, one place I could never reach. I simply had to stand back amazed and trust Him. By closing her up with Himself, God prepared Lauren so thoroughly in that summer to stand alone as a Christian, that we never worried about her giving up her faith on a very secular college campus that fall!

"You hem me in—behind and before," said David. "You have laid Your hand upon me. Such knowledge is too wonderful for me, too lofty for me to attain" (Psalm 139:5-6).

131

Most of us have experienced God's process of "hemming in" our own lives, but we are slow to recognize it in our children's lives.

After weeks of time alone with her Lord, Lauren emerged rather suddenly, quite well again, a new person. Gone was the fretfulness over her future, the desire for everything to work out according to her own plans. Instead, a quietness and confidence began to show, the kind described in Isaiah 30:15, "In repentance and rest is your salvation, in quietness and trust is your strength." When she was ready to leave, we were confident that God would continue His parenting process. What a reason to give thanks!

It is often in the darkest hours when we finally release our sweaty grip on our children's lives. What parent really has the resources of love and perfect understanding, the limitless wisdom it takes to shepherd a young person into completeness? Certainly I don't, and I would guess that you don't, either. I thank the Lord that He continues to guide and instruct, to shepherd them as only He can. Not only do His lessons reach their deepest needs, but His leading is always in the right direction! God's faithfulness to take up the parenting where we falter gives us promise and hope, and a great measure of mental rest.

As we release them, God begins His process of healing their inner person. In our children's hearts are private worlds where mothers are never invited. We can create a warm and loving environment, and be committed prayer warriors on their behalf, but Jesus, the Master Rebuilder, is the only one who can fully restore their broken worlds.

What parent with a critically ill child hasn't wrestled with the pain of absolute surrender? Many years ago in Baltimore we were deeply impressed with the quality of ministry of our pastor and his wife, Jan and Ruth Senneker. I remember the evening they both gave moving testimonies to a group of young couples. Jan told a heartbreaking story about his childhood during the Nazi occupation of the

Netherlands and of God's hand of protection on his family.

It was Ruth's story, however, that particularly touched my heart. As a child, she had been chronically ill. Her parents were devout believers who had committed each of their several children to the Lord. Ruth's health seemed to fail year by year, leaving doctors baffled about how to help her. They were certain the problem was her heart.

Ruth's brokenhearted mother could no longer stand by and watch her daughter dying, and cried out in prayer one day, "Take her, Lord! She's Yours! But if You can use her in Your kingdom, let her live!"

Soon afterward, a young intern at the hospital spoke up to the doctors, telling them that he felt Ruth's case had been wrongly diagnosed. Instead of a heart problem, he was certain the problem was her lungs. He was right! With correct treatment, Ruth gained quickly in strength, and eventually grew into a godly woman.

After Ruth and Jan were married, they spent several fruitful years as missionaries in Australia before coming to our church. Jan prayed fervently for my husband's conversion to Christ, and quietly led Steve to the Lord on Halloween evening, 1972. A few years later we learned the tragic news that their two oldest children had been killed by a car while waiting for the school bus. I have often thought how costly their ministry for the kingdom of God has been, and yet how safe at the same time. Every great offering is safest when it is in God's keeping. Only in God's kingdom do we gain by letting go.

Second Gear

Every mother on earth has said under her breath, "I can hardly wait until these children are out of the house!" Usually, they begin the refrain secretly, when their children are small fry bringing toads into the kitchen, whining at ten o'clock in the morning that there's nothing to do, or layering the living room with Legos. Kindergarten never looked more inviting than on those extra long days with four-year-olds. Yet, when school days finally arrive, we walk from room to room, missing them. The adjustment can be surprisingly difficult.

Eventually, the day comes when every one is grown up and independent. (I use both terms loosely.) The house is yours again, as are all those hours you dreamed of over the last twenty or so years when bedlam reigned at times, or tensions were high, and energy at an all-time low. Was it all worth it? Some women really wonder.

A few years ago I overheard a mother bitterly lament, "I put too much into my mothering! I did too much for them, and what did I get back? Nothing but heartache and grief! None of them appreciate all I did, the way I worked and sacrificed. None of them turned out the way I had hoped. If you want children, spare yourself the trouble and go out and buy a doll or raise dogs instead! They don't turn on you!"

"Ouch!" I thought to myself. "Could her children really be as bad as all that? Why is she so bitter?" As I matured as a mother and experienced some hard times myself, I realized that a lot of that woman's bitter attitude came from a refusal to accept the painful process it often takes for children to reach maturity. Rather, she focused all her efforts on raising children who would please her, meet all her expectations, and not cause her undue grief. As many of us know, that is simply not the case. Children are not given to us to meet those needs; they are here to glorify God. All the experiences of mothering, the joys as well as the sorrows, the stretching experiences that consumed us at the time represent the arduous effort, similar to birth pains, needed to bring forth a new generation.

Wrestling with relationships within the home happens to be part of mothering. Sometimes, it's because a child needs more personal attention, or because he wants more independence and privileges and it's hard for a mother to let go. Our instincts can bring us to quick judgments that may be hurtful and incorrect. I approached my friend,

Jewel Hubley, for advice in just such a matter.

"There are many solutions to a problem," she reminded me kindly, "but next to love, anything else is only second best." I can't tell you how many times her words have returned to me over the years. Our focus should be on pleasing God, loving as He loved, especially when it's hard, regardless of the cost. And when the mothering is done, may we lay it down at His feet with a prayer,

> Here they are, Lord, the children you have given me.
> I release them one last time to You.
> Please forgive all my failures, blow them away like chaff
> and let the good You've given them always stay in their hearts.
> Make these children men and women after Your own heart.
> And now use me any way You choose in your kingdom.

The mother who finally lets her children's lives rest securely in God's care, is a mother who finds herself released to live and to serve Him in a new way.

SIXTEEN

THE GENERATIONAL EFFECT

On my mother's bookshelf one day I discovered two tattered books, a Bible and a small book of Psalms. A guest speaker in our high school many years ago used them to illustrate the true story of a family who traveled by covered wagon across our state two hundred years ago, facing hardships unknown to us today. It was a moving and inspirational message. After he spoke, Mother found the two ancient books in her classroom. She contacted the gentleman right away, saying, "I have your books! I don't know why, but they're here and I'd like to return them to you."

"It must be some mistake, Madam," he replied. "I have my two books right here in front of me."

Since that day, my mother has believed in the supernatural.

I love old things that tell a story, don't you? Even the hundred-year-old maples that lined the streets of our small hometown fascinated me because of the generations who had passed beneath them. And so, I opened that old Bible and psalter with delight. How I would love to have talked with their owners!

Both books had old leather covers that hung by a thread.

Pages had long since fallen out of them. But carefully enclosed in the heavy leaves of the old Bible were a few glimpses of its owner.

First, two fabric scraps fell out, perhaps samples to remember a favorite dress or a quilt that was once made. Next, I found a newspaper clipping dated 1865, a letter, and a faded page recording the birth of three children in the 1840s in western New York state. Gently, I handled the feather-light letter. In it were recorded the ages and birthdates of the writer's parents and eleven brothers and sisters in 1843. Two had died in early childhood. A brief note followed:

Our ages here are just as Father and Mother told me in 1843 and I think they are all correct. [They were both seventy-four years old, and most of the children had reached middle age.]

O how glad I would be if I could go in and sit down with you all and have a good talk instead of trying to write. I suppose Mattie has written all, but I must say a few words. You cannot think how much we have thought of you since we were there and especially since we heard of your deep affliction. We can sympathize with you, but our only hope is in God. He is our only refuge and in Him may we trust, and by and by we shall meet our loved ones in that happy land above, where sickness, sorrow, pain, and death are feared and felt no more.

Last, I read the newspaper clipping, which contained a piece of original poetry entitled "Light in Darkness" by Mr. and Mrs. H.C. Carrington. The poem is too lengthy to quote, but the message, clothed with an olden grace, was a clear word of comfort to bereaved parents whose "little lambs" had been called home early by the Master.

It was a moving experience, looking back into the life of a family over a century ago, feeling their pain at losing a child. Then, turning back to reality, I said to myself, "Virelle, don't you realize that they're all gone now, all eleven children, their parents, and even those three babies whose birthdays are recorded here? Every memory of them is gone, except these few scraps of cloth, these faded pages in an old Bible. This is all there is left of a whole family! Someday, our own family will all be gone too, and what will be left?" It was a sobering thought, and brought a few tears as I considered the relentless passing of time.

Right on its heels followed another thought, and I remembered the words in the note: "He is our only refuge . . . we shall meet our loved ones . . . where sickness, sorrow, pain, and death are feared and felt no more." Like a light turning on in my head, I knew for a fact that those family members who were bound by the love of Christ were also bound eternally together with Him. Safe and secure, away from the trials and sadness they had faced settling a wilderness, they were now together at home with their Lord. And why? Because some faithful mother and father cherished the children God had loaned to them, and passed along their faith and knowledge of Him.

Translated for me, that meant I needed to develop some of the same qualities of those early settlers, namely faith, tenacity, and a love that simply wouldn't let go, no matter what happens. Can it be that the strength of our family's next generation could depend to a large extent on the way I live my life now, the way I mother my children, the way I love others? I believe it can.

The current pulling us away from God grows stronger. Christian mothers need to tighten their grip on those values held most dear. For me, that means love for God evidenced in faithful devotion to both my husband and children, a strong sense of loyalty to my Christian family, and an enduring faith in God's character and His Word.

The strength of our grip comes not from our particular abilities, our impressive knowledge of the Word, or our service to others, but rather from the steady certainty within us of God's love, His ability to keep His promises, and the joy of obeying Him each day as we carry out our service for Him. Central to every matter should be our desire to please God.

Jesus laid it on the line when He said, "Wide is the gate and broad is the road that leads to destruction, and many enter through it. But small is the gate and narrow the road that leads to life, and only a few find it" (Matthew 7:13-14). Surely we have all felt the swelling current that threatens to carry us all toward the wider gate. Christian mothers are in a unique position to speak to the heart of a new generation and lead it back onto God's path. We must never, never let go of the children He has given, the faith He has granted us, and the opportunities we have day after day to reach out to those who touch our lives. The heritage we will hand to the next generation is the family likeness of Christ in God's children.

Who's Modeling Whom?
How loosely society defines mothering! The mother's role has been melted down to a generic care-giver. Anyone can fit the description: fathers, daycare providers, nannies, brothers, sisters, or grandparents. In fact, one father I met told me proudly, "I know just what it's like to be a mother! My wife had twins and I took a lot of time off from work to help her!" Hurray for daddies that help, but we all know that's not the whole of mothering.

Just as loosely defined is the family. Now looked upon more as a group of people under one roof, the family has become a form without a head or heart, without hands to serve or feet to carry it in one direction. What is frightening to me is that the Christian home so often models the secular home in that its greatest effort is simply to maintain and feed itself rather than to reach out in love to a needy world.

A few years ago I experienced this in our own family. I

had taken a half-time teaching job to help with college tuition costs. I enjoyed it immensely, as I had a few other times when I had substituted for brief periods. But very soon my schedule began to revolve around nothing but maintenance. Each day before and after school I had a limited amount of time to accomplish all the shopping, cooking, cleaning, and chauffering that needed to be done. Every family member helped, and we managed quite well, except for two things. Gone was the time for regular friendships; seldom was I able to even visit with my mother. Secondly, there was no time or energy left for helping others with their needs. Our own family's needs simply had to come first in order to survive. What a shallow life it proved to be, living only to maintain ourselves.

What should stand out in a Christian home is not that we are as comfortable as other people, but that the home is filled with love. If there is no evidence of God's wisdom in the choices we make, the entertainment we choose, the way we spend our money, even the way we conduct ourselves in dealings with our neighbors, then something is gravely wrong. If your children's friends think you're harsh, grouchy, or unapproachable, what ministry will you ever have to them? When your children reflect your ways (and you can be sure they will!) what will be evident—your kindness, acceptance, forgiveness, and patience or their opposites? Can your children and their friends honestly believe what you say about Jesus Christ because they see Him alive in your home? I ask myself the same questions daily.

The Family Calling
Every Christian family has a calling that is the most important part of the family heritage. God intends that the Christian home should be a blessing to the world, not just to itself. After Abraham had displayed heartbreaking obedience in his willingness to offer up his only son, Isaac, on the altar, God made a promise that carries down the centu-

ries to us—"through your offspring all nations on earth will be blessed, because you have obeyed Me" (Genesis 22:18).

Others should be drawn to Christ by what they see in the little laboratory called our family. Even through times of trial, God is proving His reality to others by our example.

Psalm 61:5 points to a treasure belonging to every Christian home: "You have given me the heritage of those who fear Your name." God creates a heritage for our children and grandchildren as a result of our faithfulness.

If you were raised in a home that honored God, you are much richer than most. If you are raising your children in a Christ-honoring home, you are enriching their lives immeasurably and providing them a heritage that they will someday pass along to their children.

My friend Kim put it this way, "I like to think that Don and I have begun a new heritage for our children. I get excited just thinking about God's faithfulness and all the ways He's going to bless the world through our children and grandchildren." I get excited thinking about it too. Kim's daughter and her husband and baby daughter have just arrived in Thailand as missionaries and her two married sons are active in various ministries. There's no limit to the ways God can bless the world because of our faithful ministry to our children.

Grandparents and the Generational Effect

Psalm 145:4 tells us, "One generation will commend Your works to another; they will tell of your mighty acts." One of the ways one generation speaks to the next is through the significant relationships children have with their grandparents. How blessed my children have been to have enjoyed the love of three grandparents all their lives. I never had that privilege. Grandparents are often great storytellers and should be encouraged to tell and retell stories of God's faithfulness to family members, how He helped them through times of suffering and adversity, and filled their lives with meaning and purpose. One family I know has recorded their grandparents' testimonies on tape. We have some wonderful books in which each of our grandparents have answered interesting questions about their lives. Each grandparent has impacted our children's lives permanently, and we are all richer for it.

Of all the grandmothers in the Bible, who can compare with Naomi, mother-in-law of Ruth? I've long been impressed with this woman of faith and tenacity. She simply would not let go of what God had given her, even when things looked pretty dim.

Naomi was an Israelite whose husband brought her, along with their two sons, to live in the country of Moab because of the famine in their own land. There both sons married Moabite women, Orpah and Ruth. Within ten years, all three men had died, leaving Naomi, Orpah, and Ruth widowed and without resources. Naomi determined to return to her homeland where it was rumored there was now a season of plenty. She urged both daughters-in-law to return to Moab and their own families with her blessing. Orpah bade her farewell, but Ruth clung to her in a dramatic statement of deep devotion saying, "Where you go I will go, where you stay I will stay. Your people will be my people and your God my God" (Ruth 1:16).

After they returned to Israel, Naomi guided Ruth to glean in the fields of Boaz, her kinsman, hoping he would fulfill the role of kinsman-redeemer and marry Ruth. The love story of Ruth and Boaz is a tender one in the way it mingles righteousness and compassion, humility and trust. Their first child, Obed, entered into the line of the Messiah. Not only was Naomi a joyous grandmother who preserved her husband's family line, but she became a blessing to succeeding generations.

Redeeming a Generation
It may be difficult to realize it at times, but the effects of our lives will really last for generations. The quality of our

mothering will impact those yet unborn. Much like Naomi's faithful grip on God's promises, we need the same sense that what we do today really matters in God's plan, not just for ourselves, but for the lives of many others as well.

God gave me an illustration one day out of my memory bank that helped me understand the whole matter a little better. I remembered a camping trip we made with friends in Maryland, when we spent a warm afternoon hiking up the rocky edges of a beautiful creek. We all took off our shoes, and waded through the deliciously cool water that bounced around the rocks. Steve, following his fisherman instincts, adventured a little farther toward the middle of the creek where the water was deeper. Slipping on a mossy rock, he was suddenly swept downstream by a powerful current. I'd love to tell you we all went to his rescue, but the truth is, no one even noticed his absence. Steve was too surprised to say anything, and too busy trying to grab another rock or a branch even to think of yelling for help. It wasn't until he dragged himself out of the water and came up behind us on the path, drenched and bruised, that we learned what had happened to him. Imagine how guilty we all felt!

Much like our adventure that day, today's young people are also dabbling in waters they are unfamiliar with, waters of self-indulgence and sensuousness. Some are already perched in slippery places near the dangerous rocks of disillusionment and despair. Worse still, some have already been swept downstream, and we haven't even heard their cry.

None of us doubts the presence today of a swift and godless current that threatens to sweep away the faith and moral fiber of a whole generation. But we never expect our own children to be pulled into it. Sometimes we hardly even notice it's happening until it's too late.

I firmly believe Christian mothers have been given a special opportunity to reach out in God's strength and love, with an arm to rescue many precious young people from the slippery path to destruction. But first we need to hear their cry.

Reach Out and Touch Someone

Until Christ returns, He heads an unbroken chain of love from the strong reaching out to help the weak. How would any of us have found Christ if it were not for someone reaching out to us? Whom has God given you to hang on to? Ask Him to give you one more, perhaps a young person needing a friend, or a place to live; perhaps another mother needing encouragement and help. With one arm, care for your own, and with the other, reach out and help another. It is the Lord Jesus Himself who heads this chain of love, and He never lets go. As you trust the strength of His grip, hold on tightly to those He has given you, and don't let go of them, either. Together we will grow into one great family of God and faithfully pass on the likeness of Christ to the next generation.

"The light that shines furthest is the brightest at home."[1] Home is a beacon shining down from one generation to another, lighting the way for those who would follow. Mothers are to tend that light for their children's safe passage into adulthood. In doing so, they preserve a heritage of those who honor His name above all names, and bring the blessing of Abraham to a lost world.

ACKNOWLEDGMENTS

My deepest gratitude goes to my loving husband, Steve, and supportive family at home: Amy, Dave, and Bob, who "believed in Mom" these last few months, learned to live without homemade cookies, and never complained when their clothes disappeared for weeks into the ironing or mending pile. I love you all! Special thanks to our daughter, Lauren, and her husband Mike, for their tireless encouragement, cute cards, and the words, "Go, Mom!" in the margins. And to my own dear mom, thank you for skillful editing and support beyond the call of duty.

To my fantastic friends, Judie, Lorraine, Linda, Ruth, and others who appear in this book, I offer my thanks for being women whose counsel and example I treasure. You have given me more than I can ever hope to return.

A special word of thanks to Carole Streeter, my editor, for taking time to come and visit me, helping me bring into focus what was on my heart, and believing I could do it.

Most of all, I thank my Father in heaven, for His everlasting patience and kindness, and for not giving up on me yet.

Virelle Kidder

NOTES

Chapter 1
1. Seamands, David, *Healing Grace* (Wheaton, Illinois: Victor Books, 1988), 19.

Chapter 2
1. Schaeffer, Edith, *What Is a Family?* (Old Tappan, New Jersey: Fleming H. Revell, 1975), 119.
2. Lewis, C.S., *Mere Christianity* (New York: Macmillan, 1943), 55.

Chapter 4
1. Taylor, Kenneth, *The Bible in Pictures for Little Eyes* (Chicago: Moody Press, 1956).

Chapter 5
1. Lewis, C.S., "The Chronicles of Narnia Super-Soundbook" (London: Caedmon, 1982).

Chapter 7
1. Schultz, Charles, "Peanuts," *Schenectady Gazette* (April 25, 1989).
2. Campbell, Ross, *How to Really Love Your Child* (Wheaton, Illinois: Victor Books, 1980), 104-105.

Chapter 9
1. Mowday, Lois, "Naive No Longer," an interview, *Today's Christian Woman* (May/June 1989), 42.

Chapter 11
1. Dobson, James, *Dr. Dobson Answers Your Questions* (Wheaton, Illinois: Tyndale House, 1988), 201.
2. Jensen, Margaret, *Lena* (San Bernardino, California: Here's Life, 1985).

Chapter 12
1. Graham, Ruth Bell, *Sitting By My Laughing Fire* (Waco, Texas: Word, 1977), 159

Chapter 13
1. Salomon, Janet Lynn, "Motherhood: No Medals but Many Lasting Rewards," an interview, *Decision* (May 1989), 17.
2. *Ibid.*, 16.
3. Bounds, E.M., *Winning the Invisible War* (Springdale, Pennsylvania: Whitaker House, 1984), 72.
4. Dobson, James, *Dr. Dobson Answers Your Questions* (Wheaton, Illinois: Tyndale House, 1988), 259.

Chapter 14
1. Graham, Ruth Bell, *Sitting By My Laughing Fire* (Waco, Texas: Word, 1977), 117.
2. Camp, Ruth, notes from a ladies retreat, Word of Life, Schroon Lake, New York; May 1989.
3. Edman, V. Raymond, *In Quietness and Confidence* (Wheaton, Illinois: Scripture Press, 1953), 63.

Chapter 16
1. Wiersbe, Warren, "Back to the Bible," a radio broadcast, March 9, 1989.